Next Year I'll Be Famous

Be Famous

Almost Making it in the Music Business... over Six Hilarious Decades!

Brian Flockhart

Next Year I'll Be Famous

Cover design by Steven Suttie

Font type Book Antiqua

P/B 1st Edition – published 15th March 2019
Kindle 1st Edition – published 15th March 2019

Thank you to my long-suffering partner Janet, who finally talked me into writing about all of my experiences in bands and the entertainment business after hearing all about the varied tales and situations that I have found myself in through the years.

Thank you also to all of the characters who appear in this book, and those that I have met along the way, all of whom have made this book possible.

Many thanks to Steven Suttie whom without his expertise and help, this book would not have seen the light of day.

Preface

Brian "Brick" Flockhart was born in 1946 in Edinburgh, and was, in his own words, lucky to be at the right place, right time, when the most exciting period of music in Britain was in its infancy. At this time, The Beatles and the Rolling Stones were starting out on their incredible rollercoaster of a musical ride. What followed was a revolution in British music and Brian was lucky enough to be on board for the entire ride.

Come with him on his own trip, as he travels through many experiences, funny and otherwise over a 50-year journey of highs and lows in the entertainment industry.

Chapter One
A Star is born

"We could do that," said Jimmy.

"Do what?" I asked. We were at a local youth club and there was a beat group playing on stage.

"We could do that", repeated Jimmy, nodding towards the stage.

"You mean learn to play music," I asked.

"Yeh, start a band up."

To put you in the picture, it was the early sixties, and the Beatles, and the Liverpool sound had just exploded on to the music scene.

"Just look at all the birds hanging around the stage, it's like flies around shit," grinned our James, "and not one of these bastards are anything to look at," he added.

"So, you want to get a band together?"

"Yeh, I think it's a great idea, and think of all these eager females," Jimmy replied.

"Well, apart from the fact that we haven't played a guitar in our lives, there are only two of us and we ain't exactly film star material ourselves, I think it could work," I replied sarcastically.

"Well there's Rob and Michael over there, I bet they would give it a go," said Jimmy, referring to two of our mates on the other side of the dance floor. "I'm gonna ask them." And with that he was off. Jimmy was the kind of guy that, when he had an idea, it had to be seen to right away. Within two minutes he was back. "Good news, my sceptical friend, they are both up for it, and Rob's brother has a guitar he doesn't use any more."

"One guitar between four people doesn't exactly make a band, does it?" I said.

"Look, I said we would meet up tomorrow and talk about it, sort of see how it will go," he answered.

"Ok", I sighed, "we'll meet up at your house tomorrow then", resigning myself to his persistence.

"Yeah, that's what I wanted to hear!" beamed Jimmy, "now let's get back to the more important things at present, like woo-me-n!" he howled, and with that he began earnestly scanning the dance floor to see which lovely maiden he hoped to "deflower" that night.

The next day saw four young lads caught up in the excitement of actually forming a band. Much was discussed and many problems were solved. Jimmy and Mike would play guitars, Rob would go on the drums and I would be on the bass. Musical equipment was (and still is), very expensive and we were all around sixteen years old, with trade apprenticeships, which meant that money was very scarce.

We decided that we would approach our parents and hope that they would buy the equipment we needed. We would then dutifully pay them back when we were rich and famous. (A sound and logical plan, we all agreed.) We left Jimmy's house in a buzz of excitement and went our separate ways to put the plan into action.

As I drew nearer my home, my excitement waned considerably, as it would mean asking my father for something that he, (I was assuming) would be totally against.

My dear old dad was a strict but fair man, spending the Second World War in the army, leaving with the rank of sergeant in the Royal Scots regiment. He was a "no frills attached" type of man, plus the fact that we didn't have much money to spare and what we had, was usually put to practical use.

As I opened the door, I had visions of him yelling at me to "not be so daft", when I asked him to buy me a guitar.

"Hi dad!" I called brightly, trying to act nonchalant.

"Hi son," he replied. He was sitting in his usual chair, with the Sunday paper in front of him, legs stretched out by the fire. Mum was in the kitchen, cremating the Sunday lunch (as usual.) There was never a dull moment at mealtimes in our house, with the favourite pastime of "guess what's on the plate" a regular occurrence! Needless to say, over the years, we were resigned to the fact that she was not the best of cooks.

"Dad, me and the lads have been talking, and we were thinking of starting a band." I blurted out. (SILENCE) "We wouldn't need much, just a guitar and stuff." I continued, hopefully. (LONGER SILENCE) "The thing is, I haven't got enough money to buy it at the moment. (Translated as no money at all) But Jimmy and Mike's parents are buying them theirs," I lied, "and Rob's dad is buying him his drums," I lied some more.

The paper came down from the front of his face very slowly, and he stared at me with a questioning look.

"How much do these guitar thingies cost?" he asked.

Damn! I hadn't expected him to ask that! I was fully prepared for him to dismiss the whole thing and this question threw me off guard. (Plus I hadn't a clue of the price of them guitar thingies.)

"It'll be about ten or fifteen pounds," I said, taking a stab at the cost.

"That's a lot of money son," he mused. "And you say that the rest of the parents are buying their stuff for them?" he asked.

"Yes dad", (lying once more.)

"Ok then, we'll get together with them and go to Edinburgh at the weekend and get what you need."

This was a severe shock to my system! My dad! My strict, but fair dad was going to buy me a guitar, no questions asked! WOW! I rushed round to Jimmy's house to tell him the news. When I arrived, Mike and Rob were there as well.

All our folks had said yes!

It had turned out they had used the same story as I had. No matter, (as long as we were not found out!)

We were on our way to fame and fortune.

Chapter Two
The Smell of the Crowd

As it turned out, the following Saturday, all the dads would come with us to buy the equipment. The shop we had selected was down an old cobbled street just off the Grass Market area called Coburn Street.

The Grass Market was renowned as a hangout for wino's and drug addicts, (an auspicious start for us aspiring superstars.) The shop itself was surprisingly small, or perhaps it felt small due to the fact that it was crammed with every piece of musical instrument and equipment imaginable. It was like a musical "hanging garden of Babylon," with guitars, trombones, trumpets, violins, in fact every conceivable piece of musical equipment, all dangling on metal hooks from the ceiling. So, by the time parents, and future rock stars entered, there was precious little room left.

"There's no one here," said Jimmy.

"Press the bell." I said, and having done so, a shuffling sound could be heard coming from the rear of the shop. What emerged was a cross between Shylock, Uriah Heap and Ebenezer Scrooge.

"What can I do for you?" he asked in a tired voice, his bushy eyebrows crossed in an irritated frown. "We'd like to buy some guitars, oh! And some drums as well." Said Jimmy, excitedly.

Ebenezer's face suddenly lit up in a beaming smile as he walked around the counter to greet us.

"Starting a band are we?" he asked.

"Yes!" we all answered together.

"Well you've come to the right place for all you will need", he announced. "Now, let's start with a look at the guitars", he said. "We have some nice Fenders here at the very reasonable price of around one hundred pounds or so." He must have seen the stunned look in all our faces, (particularly the dads), as he hurriedly followed up with "but if that's too much, we have some over here at around thirty pounds, quite reasonable, but still a very nice guitar to play."

That was double what I had expected my Dad to pay, and my heart began to sink. I looked at him, and he gave me a quick nod in reply. The other two also got the nod from their dads, so we were in business.

A drum kit was selected for Rob, and three small amplifiers for the guitars quickly chosen. The deal was done! The shop owner's face had a look of rapture, as each dad lined up and counted out the money and handed it over. (No credit cards in those days).

As we left the shop, we looked at each other with wild excitement. This was it! We were a real band now, with all the gear needed to start out, (even though we couldn't play a single note between us).

Only Rob was not caught up in the mood as much as the rest of us, as he realised that playing drums meant carrying a lot of little drums, big drums, stands and so on. His father was feeling the same, as they staggered to his car laden with all the baggage that it involved.

When I got home, I couldn't wait to get started, and was heading for my room with my shiny new guitar, when my dad stopped me.

"So, the guitar and amplifier comes to about sixty pounds," he said, looking thoughtfully at the ceiling. "And how much do you make a week?" he asked.

"About two pounds and ten shillings." I replied. (Apprentice wages have always been very low.)

"And how much do you pay mum for your lodgings?" he asked again.

"A pound", I answered.

"And how much for the bus fares to work?" he persisted.

"Ten shillings", I told him.

"Right!" he said, "I'll take ten Bob a week until you have paid for everything, that leaves you ten shillings to get by on, so you'll have to learn how to play the damn thing, because you can't afford to do anything else!" (Sigh, my father, my strict but fair father).

We had managed to find a place to rehearse in the local gym at nights. It felt strange to set our gear up in the middle of a boxing ring, with the smell of sweat and embrocating oil lingering in the air from the day's exertions of the boxers, but it served our purpose.

In the months that followed, we practiced hard and the weird plonks and twang noises we made at the start eventually developed into vaguely sounding like chart hits. (When I say vague, I mean vague!)

We had also acquired some microphones and speakers, or a P.A. system as it was called, from a friend. So, on the whole, we were fully equipped. (Minus the musical ability!).

As we prepared for a rehearsal one evening, Jimmy came rushing in, full of excitement. "Guess what men; I've got us a gig!"

"Where?" we all cried in unison.

"In the Casino", he answered.

"But we only know eight numbers!" I said.

"Yeah, but we only have to do about forty minutes or so, cos' it's an audition." He replied.

"When is it then?" Rob asked.

"It's a week on Friday!" Answered Jimmy and a buzz of excitement enveloped us as we knuckled down to rehearse with a new purpose.

Our first gig! "Wait a minute." Said Mike. "How are we going to get our gear there?"

"Simple", said Jimmy, "we'll take it on

the bus!"

And that is exactly what we did.

As we got off the bus on that Friday night with all our gear, we stood outside "The Casino" with mixed feelings, ranging from heart pulsing excitement, to gut wrenching fear. Only Rob was not completely swept up in the spirit of it all as the conductor on the bus had charged him for three fares, as his drums had taken up so much room.

"Cost me one and six", he grumbled. "Never mind", Mike said, "you can take it out of our first million!" He joked.

We looked at "The Casino" entrance. This was it, our first steps on the stairway to fame.

The name "The Casino" sounded very swish and swanky but in actual fact, it was a converted picture house. It had two rooms. The main room was filled with poker and blackjack tables, and a rather tatty looking roulette wheel. Beyond that was the dance hall, with a raised platform at the end for the band.

In front of the "stage," on the floor, was what looked like drainage system running the full length of the room! (We later found out that this was to enable the blood and beer to flow away from the dance floor after the frequent fights!)

The owner had the bright idea, that once a gambler had spent all his cash at the tables, he could enter the dance area for free and have a drink on the house. Considering the guys had mostly come straight from work, still in their overalls and were already worse the wear for drink and dreading meeting up with their wives when they got home, this was a recipe for disaster.

Add to this, the occasional guy who actually won, and was in high spirits, plus the biggest, heaviest glass ashtrays you have ever seen, (just for ammunition) and there you have it, world war three. To sum "The Casino" up, if you have ever seen the Blues Brothers movie, imagine their gig at the sleazy bar, and that was it. (Minus the safety net!)

As we headed in through the door, we were met by a gorilla in an evening suit, who asked politely, "what the fuck do you lot want?"

"We're the band." I answered.

"Bit young for this place aren't you?"

"We've got an audition," said Jimmy. "Good luck, 'cos you'll fucking need it!" He chuckled. By good fortune the main band for the night was already there and had set up ready to play. I will always remember their kindness when they allowed us to use their equipment, which was so much better than ours.

The owner appeared and asked, "You the new lot?"

"Yes," we replied.

"You're on at nine, off at nine-thirty, okay and if you are shite I will drag you off before that!"

The main band kicked off, and we began to have second thoughts about the whole idea. Damn! They were pretty good.

We sat round a table near to the stage and watched the big clock on the far wall, edging closer to the dreaded nine o'clock. The band finished the last number of their first set and all too soon it was our turn.

"Right boys!" Said Jimmy, "It's shit or bust time." I can't remember much of that half hour, only that the hall was pretty empty, but those who were there gave us a clap after every number.

Then, as quickly as it had begun, it was over. The owner, who had been watching, walked over and said, "I'll give you every fourth Friday at four pounds a night, take it or leave it." Fame – here we come! "By the way," he said, "what's your name?"

"Name?" we answered blankly.

"Yeh, the name of the band,"

"Class of sixty-one!" I blurted out. Damn! We hadn't thought of a name!

"Shit name," he called, as he wandered back to the bar.

"Class of sixty-one," Jimmy sighed, "Where did that come from?"

"Well, I had to think of something quick," I said, defending myself.

"It'll have to do for now, I suppose," he

muttered.

With that we lugged our gear on to the ten o'clock bus and headed for home.

Chapter Three
Kings of the Road

In the months that followed, 'The Casino' proved to be an excellent training experience for the four fledglings of rock that we were. We quickly learned to sense when trouble was about to start and we could pull our gear to the back of the stage when it erupted, whilst still playing. The boss had told us, "No matter what, even if someone is being murdered out there, keep playing!"

We were also getting better, and a few local venues began to book us. About this time, we lost Rob. His heart really wasn't in it and he decided that he'd had enough. His replacement was a guy called Ian, who was much more experienced, having played with a blues band for a year and this much improved the band. Ian was what I would call a 'typical drummer.' He had three loves – his drums, his drink, and his unquenchable thirst to score with every female he could get his hands on; the order of these three loves changed on a nightly basis.

Up to this point we had relied on friends and relatives to transport us to the gigs; the bus company refused to take us anymore! As the bookings were becoming further afield we seriously needed our own transport. As two of us had recently passed our driving tests and having saved up our money from our gigs – less cash to our Dads – we started to search for a van. Ian arrived one night with the news that he had found a van for us.

"How much?", we asked.

"Twenty-eight pounds and ten shillings!"

"Wow! That's cheap. Where is it?"

"It's near Dalkeith."

"What's the garage called?" I asked.

"It's not in a garage."

"So, it's at somebody's house then?" I enquired.

"Erm, not exactly," he hedged, "it's in a field."

"In a field, what's it doing in a field?"

"The owner left it there. Look, why don't we have a look at it and see what you think?"

Intrigued, we all piled into Ian's beat- up Ford Poplar and headed for Dalkeith.

What awaited us had to be seen to be believed. In the middle of a field, lying on its side, with the back doors open, and revealing horse manure piled high inside, was our 'bargain buy.'

It was a Bedford Dormobile van in a very bad state indeed... The original logo of a local bakery firm had been scraped off, and the rest of the body's green paint had been sanded down, presumably to re-paint it, but the rust had got there first.

"You are taking the piss!" cried Mike. "The farmer said he could have it up and running by tomorrow for us!" Defended Ian.

"Ian," I said, "that thing hasn't moved for years, the grass has grown halfway up its fucking sides! It's a wreck!"

"Listen, listen," said Ian. "I'm sure I could bargain with the guy and get it cheaper."

"Cheaper! I wouldn't take it if the bastard paid me," I stormed.

Just then the farmer appeared. "All right lads?" he asked, "well what do you think then?"

At that moment all we could think of was strangling Ian.

"I know she looks a bit rough, but she's got a cracking little engine in her, and I'll stick a new battery in for you." The farmer added.

"How much do you want for it," asked Ian, ignoring our frantically shaking heads.

"Twenty-eight pounds and ten shillings," came the reply.

"We'll give you twenty-two," said Ian.

"Done!" said the farmer, a little too quickly for our liking. "Come round tomorrow night, and I'll have it up and running for you, but you can't have the horse shit., that's mine!"

We left in a dark mood, with Ian being our least favourite person on the planet at that moment.

"It'll be fine, honest," he said, in a voice far from convincing.

"It had better be," said Jimmy darkly.

The next evening, we arrived at the

Farmhouse and were taken to one of the adjoining barns by the farmer. There it was. I must admit it looked a whole lot better standing on its wheels, than on its side. It was still rusty, but at least most of the manure had gone.

"Okay then," said the farmer, "I've put a battery in her, done the oil and water, so she's ready to roll, or in your case rock and roll, ha ha." He seemed quite pained when we didn't appreciate his attempt at comedy.

I jumped in and turned the ignition key. To our amazement, it started first time, and "ticked over" well. "Told you she was a good 'un," he said.

Tally-ho! We were off! And everyone piled into our very own "bandwagon."

I had to admit that it drove very well and the two sliding doors at the driver and passenger sides were an added bonus, because, as the engine warmed up, the overpowering stench of horse shit filled the interior.

"Christ, I'm gonna puke," said Jimmy.

"It'll be ok once we've given it a good clean out, "promised Ian. As we drove along, we noticed that everyone we passed was staring at us. The cars that were passing us were slowing down to take a good look at this rusting wreck on the road.

"We're gonna have to do something with the bodywork on this thing, or the cops will be pulling us in all day!" Warned Jimmy. We all agreed, and Mike said he had some left over paint in his dad's shed we could use. As the next day was Saturday we agreed to meet on some local wasteland and give the old Bedford a "paint job and scrub." As I dropped Mike off last and set off home, I felt we were really going up in the world.

I pulled up outside my house and slid the van door back, jumped out, and gave the bonnet a pat. I turned round and came face to face with my father, who, judging by the scowling expression on his face, was not in the best of moods.

"What the hell is that?" he demanded.

"That's our new group van," I said proudly.

"Group van, I've seen better on the top pile in scrap merchants!" He yelled. "It's not staying here," he added. "You're not leaving that thing outside my door!"

I looked at him pleadingly, "but dad, where else can I park it?"

"Around by the old abandoned garages, but it's not staying here," he repeated. "And what's that bloody awful smell?"

Saturday came, and we descended on the waste ground, armed with paint and brushes, ready for the "makeover."

"What colours have you got?" I asked.

"I've got some black and white," said Mike.

"That'll be eye catching," smirked Ian.

"First of all gents, its shift the shit time," said Jimmy.

We set to work, and two hours later (and two gallons of disinfectant,) we had the interior in a reasonable condition. (We could never quite get rid of the smell of that horse shit and even when the old Dormobile went to the great scrap yard in the sky, a year later, there was still a lingering trace of it).

Next came the paint job. The four of us bent to the task and within an hour, there it stood in all its glory, a sleek black mean machine.

"What'dya think?" asked Jimmy.

"It looks like a fucking hearse," replied Ian.

"The name has still to go on." I said. (By this time, we were calling ourselves "The Manner").

"Right, who's the Picasso between us," asked Jimmy.

"I'll give it a go," I said, and set to work with the white paint.

Quite soon, on both sides of the van "The Manner" stood out boldly.

"Not bad Bricky boy, not bad at all!" Praised Jimmy.

"Still too plain," moaned Ian. "Why don't we paint some teeth on the grill, and eyes on the bonnet," he suggested.

This was duly done, followed by a "wot, no engine" logo, with a face peering over a brick wall on the cowling.

"I've got an idea," said Ian, taking his shoes off. "I'll dip my feet in the paint, and walk up the sides of the van, if you all hold me up."

Agreed.

"How about a hand at each side on the back, with the message, "push here," suggested Mike.

Agreed.

The final touch to the masterpiece was a logo which read; "don't laff lady, your daughter may be in here!" This was written on each side. We stood back, admiring our handy work. God, it looked great!

After a few hours to let the paint dry off a bit, we decided to take our work-of-art for a spin. As we drove through our home town of Musselburgh, we seemed to be causing quite a stir amongst the locals.

This time, as our van passed the people on the pavements, they were staring in disbelief, rather than pity.

"Rock on," said Ian. "The natives will certainly notice us now, we're getting a lot of attention, and that means publicity."

Perhaps we were drawing too much attention, as a few minutes later we were pulled over to the side of the road by a traffic police car.

"Driver's license," the officer demanded,

in a dry voice. I dutifully handed over the document for inspection.

"Just passed your test I see," he noticed.

"Yes, and the vans taxed and tested and everything," I added helpfully.

"I didn't ask you for that," came the icy reply, "what's all this nonsense painted on the vehicle?" he asked, leaning casually against the side of the van.

"Well, we're a band and we wanted to get noticed and stick out from the crowd."

While all this was going on, the other cop had been going around the van, kicking tyres, checking the tax disc and all the usual carry-on. As he reached his mate, he gave a shrug to suggest that was in a reasonable state and walked back to the police car.

"Right!" Said our less than friendly Bobby, "you certainly stick out from the crowd alright, but if I were you lot, I'd tone it down a bit, or the other traffic cops will have a field day with you. So, on your way then."

As he walked back to his car, we noticed a large streak of black paint down the side of his immaculate white shirt, where he had been leaning against the van. We drove off as quickly as we could without causing suspicion and took the first available exit off the main road. I dropped the guys off and drove back to my house and went inside. My mum peered out of the window at the van and looked at me with a worried expression.

"What do you think then, mum?" I asked.

"It's different!" She replied and hurried back to the safety of her kitchen. Just then I heard my dad's car coming up the road and went to meet him. As he got out of his car, he stared long and hard at the vision (eyesore) in front of him and raised his eyes to the heavens.

"I preferred it the rusty way it was," he muttered. As he strode towards the house, he turned and pointing a finger at me, said "it's not staying here!"

Time passed, and the old Dormobile began to pay its way, as more and more gigs came in. As we improved and gained a foothold on the local circuit, we were able to say goodbye to the "Casino." This was a relief to us all, as it seemed only a matter of time before one of us would get hurt in one of the frequent brawls that occurred in the place.

We were playing more and more in the Edinburgh area by now. The music scene in the city at this time was buzzing, with at least forty to fifty venues for live bands. We had also recruited two male singers to the band, Calum and Peter. Surprisingly as it sounds, this combination worked very well for a short time. We managed to get a gig at the best venue in town, supporting one of the most popular local bands. This would be a huge feather in our caps, and if we did well, could lead to better things.

We arrived early in the afternoon (being Saturday) and set up. The place had a huge stage with cages at each end where the professional girl dancers gyrated to the music. It could hold about seven hundred people, and at weekends, it was the place to be.

About two hours before we were due to go on, Calum had a bad case of nerves. He decided he needed a couple of drinks to steady himself. After he had been gone an hour, I began to get worried, thinking he had "bottled it" and had gone home. Pete saw how worried I looked and volunteered to go find him.

With ten minutes to go before we were due on, the DJ told me in no uncertain terms that if we didn't get our arses up on that stage on time, he would rip our dicks off. (Charming fellow.)

I rushed out of the hall in a blind panic and looked frantically up and down the street. There they were, arm in arm, singing at the top of their voices, blind drunk!

"Jesus!" I cried. "Where the hell have you two been?"

"We've just had a couple to loosen up the vocal chords man." Slurred Cal.

"Loosen your chords!" I yelled, "You're both pissed out of your heads! Come on!" I ordered, as I pushed them through the stage doors. "We're on in two minutes."

I rushed them up the steps and onto the

stage just as the DJ was announcing us.

Whether it was luck, or drunken self-confidence, or a mixture of both, but the two of them sang really well, strutting around the stage like seasoned professionals. The rest of us played just as well and at the end of our set, got a great reception from the crowd. Even the DJ (he of the dick ripping threat) congratulated us.

"Right you two", I said, "sit here by the stage door, and don't move while I get the van and get you home." It was obvious by looking at the two of them, that the drink was really starting to kick in as they swayed unsteadily, while holding on to each other with silly grins on their faces.

The rest of us went to get the van, which was parked just a few hundred yards up the road. As we drove down, the front doors of the dance hall suddenly flew open, and two bodies came flying out, tumbling over and over, eventually lying on their backs in the middle of the street, laughing deliriously.

Oh no!, it was our terrible twins!

"What happened?" I asked.

"These two guys told us to move, so we sorted them out!" Chuckled Pete.

"Those two guys were the doormen you pricks!"

To this day, we have the dubious honour of being the only band to play "The Chase" and be banned for life for fighting with the staff!

Things began to deteriorate with the band after that episode and after a few weeks, Jimmy decided he was giving up. This came as a big shock to me, as he had always been the one with the most energy and enthusiasm.

Two days after that, Mike said he had had enough as well. So there it was, - the end. There was no "falling out" or animosity, in fact we remained close friends and kept in contact for many years after, but with them leaving, it brought the curtain down on the band, and we all went our separate ways.

I began to look for another band and joined a band from South Queensferry on the other side of Edinburgh, but they were nowhere nearly as good as the band I had with Jimmy and the others. Coupled with that was the distance I had to travel to rehearse. My heart wasn't in it and I began to think of packing it all in. Just as I reached my lowest ebb, out of the blue, I was asked to join a local band called "In Sense."

I couldn't believe my luck! These guys were a really good band and already had a following of fans in the area who liked their sound. They even had a proper manager who oversaw their gigs and affairs. It was Alan the drummer who approached me. I accepted at once.

"Great," he said, "so we can start to rehearse tonight?"

"Why tonight?" I asked.

"Well, we've got two gigs at the weekend," he answered.

"This weekend!" I cried.

"Yeh," he said, "our Bass player wants to leave as soon as possible and we can't cancel.

"But that's just three days away," I spluttered.

"Don't worry, I know you can do it!" He turned to leave and said, as if it was an afterthought "we'll leave the dance routines till next week."

"Dance routines! What dance routines?" I asked.

"We do dance routines while we play, it looks great, and the audiences love it!" he answered.

Not for the first time, (or the last) I began to wonder what I had got myself into.

That night I met the rest of the band. Apart from Alan on drums, there was Pete on rhythm guitar, Jimmy on vocals and a guy called "Soapy" on lead guitar. At first I thought he was of Asian descent due to his dark skin, but I soon found out that it was his lack of personal hygiene that gave him that hue. He just never washed! (Surprisingly he didn't seem to smell.)

We got down to business, and the rehearsal went well. Alan was a good drummer who could really drive the band. Pete and "Soapy" we're excellent guitarists and Jimmy was a first class show-man, with a great voice. He was about five foot two inches tall, with an "Elvis quiff" and sideburns, which seemed strange to me as we were playing "soul music." But when we started to play, he pranced around in a manner that would have made James Brown proud.

I was soon to learn that this guy was absolutely crazy. (In a nice way.) I rehearsed non-stop with and without the band, so when Saturday finally came around, I felt I was as ready as I could be. I was pretty nervous, because the band had a reasonable following, with quite a few fans and I was the "new guy." I needn't have worried, because, after the gig, everyone came up to me and welcomed me aboard. (Including a couple of good-looking girls). I went home that night on cloud nine. I was definitely on the way up!

As I have mentioned previously, Edinburgh's music scene was very much alive and kicking at this time and, as we were one of the better bands, we were doing four gigs on a Friday night! (Yes, it seems a lot, and it was!) The night would start at Longstone Youth Club on the outskirts of the city, then on to the "Top Storey" in the town centre, followed by a trip to a village called Bonnyrigg, ten miles outside of town and finally back to "The International Club" on the famous Princess Street in the centre once more.

As you can imagine, there was not much time to hang about. To be able to do all these gigs in the time, we had a road crew of four guys to move the equipment. These unsung (and unpaid) heroes worked miracles shifting all that heavy gear and setting it up for us. After the first gig of the night, they would load the van and move to the next, while we dried off the sweat, got changed, and followed on by car. By the time we arrived at the next venue, the gear would be set up and ready to go. This was quite a feat, as "The Top Storey" club was literally the top level of an old tenement building, four flights up.

It was by accident that I found out how they managed to transport the gear so swiftly from that tricky gig. We had just finished our set there and were getting changed in the store room (and coal house) on the floor below, when I decided to go out onto the fire escape steps for some air.

"Below!" I heard a voice above me shout.

"Clear!" came a voice on the ground. A very expensive amplifier whizzed past my eyes, heading for Mother Earth.

"Below!" cried the voice above again.

"Clear!" came the answer. This time a drum in its case followed the same path as the amplifier. As I looked down, I saw the drum bounce up in the air off the four old mattresses piled high on top of each other on the ground, and then being expertly caught by one of the roadies, who then threw it to another crew member, who packed it in the van. I commended them on their labour saving initiative and at the same time, solved the mystery of the equipment going faulty on us every few gigs! Needless to say, the old tried and tested method, of carrying it down the stairs was re-introduced.

This elongated the life of our equipment immeasurably. (And drastically reduced the poor roadies!)

The "Top Storey Club" was at the top of Leith Walk, and was run by two brothers. By their own admission, all they did was gut out the top flight, put a stage in, some lights and paint the whole place Matt black. Their idea of maintenance after that, was to scrape the chewing gum off the floor every fortnight when it became difficult to walk without your shoes being sucked off your feet (not so many health and safety rules in those days.)

By contrast, "The International Club" was a much more select engagement. It had a ground floor entrance on the front, facing the castle, with three floors above. On each of these three floors was a dance hall, with stages at either end so that when one band finished at one end, another one would start up at the other immediately.

The better and more popular the band you were, the higher the floor you played on. (Personally, I think it should have been the other way around, and so did our poor road crew!)

The owner was an Italian guy called Jimmy Roshoe. He was a roly-poly, larger-than-life character, who always wore a Royal Stewart tartan jacket on dance nights. He trusted no one, and would stand at the entrance, counting the people going in and mentally tally up the cash. Woe betides the cashier if he or she didn't arrive at the same figure as Jimmy. I could be nice and say that he was careful with his money. But the truth was, he was as tight as a duck's arse.

Each week you would hear him arguing with the bands in his heavy Italian accent, saying, "boys, you're-a trying to-a make-a me a poor man!" This was always followed by his logic of "you-a think I know-a fucking nothing, well-a I tell-a you I know fuck all!" (Roughly translated that, we might think he was an idiot, but he was a lot smarter than we thought). Deep down I'm sure he did it out of devilment because we always got the amount we had agreed on previously. (All be it with the right amount of continental haggling).

Sadly, a few months later, the club suffered a major fire, which gutted the whole building and when it was rebuilt, it never really recovered, and went into decline.

As luck would have it, we had been booked to play the Friday and Saturday of that fateful weekend, but for some reason, we had taken our equipment home on the Friday, rather than leave it set up for the Saturday. (One of the few decisions that was good in my life!)

Chapter Four
Spreading My Wings

After the gigs at the weekend in Edinburgh, there were two restaurants where the bands would meet up and talk about the evening's event. There was the "Metropole" and the "Bandura." At three in the morning these places would be packed with musicians (and groupies) all chattering away.

Funnily, no one ever had a bad night. You would walk in and greet everyone by saying, "how was your gig?"

"Great", would come the reply.

"How was yours?" they would ask.

"Bombed them!" We would answer. Somebody had to be telling lies. (But never us!) I can still taste the minestrone soup that was the "Metropoles" speciality. It really was to die for.

All the bands had publicity photographs made, and they were plastered all over the walls of the restaurant. You knew you were one of the popular ones when your photo was displayed in the glass partition by the cash desk. (Ours was there, of course!)

You also found out about new venues from the other bands that came from out of town and could spread your wings further afield. It was through this method that we started to play in the border region of Scotland.

Every two weeks or so, we would play in

the border towns of Kelso, Hawick, Jedburgh, and Galashiels. They were great gigs because at that time, they were all mill towns, mainly employing women. The young men either worked on the land or had to move elsewhere for employment. This left a great shortage of abled-bodied men in the area. There were always buses coming down from Edinburgh and Glasgow, full of randy young lads out for a night of passion. It has to be said, that in many, many cases, they were never disappointed.

Being in a band meant you always got the pick of the girls. There was one major drawback to this, and it was based at "The Kings Arms" in Hawick. Here prowled a fearsome creature called "Big Aggie." She stood five foot four inches in height (and width!) with a voice that could keep the English Channel clear on a foggy night. She could beat the shit out of a team of sumo wrestlers whilst brushing her teeth. It was rumoured that she had bluffed her way into the S.A.S. but got kicked out for being mentally unstable.

Big Aggie's preference was always the guys in the bands. So, when she decided which one she fancied, she would wait until the poor guy had finished his set and then drag him off, screaming into the night and have her way with him. The pressure on the poor guy was unbelievable. Firstly, to have to rise to the occasion, so to speak, when confronted with a pasty white version of "Shrek" and then to perform to her very exacting standards, while under the threat of "a fucking good hiding" if he didn't, was a task that nobody had completed in recent living memory. On every occasion the guy would return, bruised, bloodied, and gibbering like a lunatic.

Then came the fateful night when she approached the stage as we were playing our last set.

"I'm having you", she bellowed, pointing dark nicotine stained finger at our singer.

"Okey dokey," replied our Jimmy cheerily. "I'll see you when we're finished" he said. We stared with pity in our eyes at the condemned man, who didn't seem in the slightest bit put out by it all. The set came to an end, and Big Aggie was standing by the stage steps to ensure her prey didn't escape.

"See you in a bit guys", said Jimmy, as he ambled out the door, arm in arm with his "date." We dismantled the gear and put it in the van and waited for his return, wondering if we should call a doctor, or a priest, or both.

Forty minutes passed, and then around the corner came our little pal, whistling a merry tune.

"You made it!" we cried. "You're in one piece!"

"Of course I am!" Said the happy little chappy.

"You must have been some sex machine to satisfy that beast!" Said Alan.

"Well, I can't take all the credit," breezed Jimmy, "I had a little help from my trusty friend!"

"What friend?" We asked.

"This beauty!" said Jimmy, producing the biggest dildo we had ever seen in our lives. It must have been eighteen inches long, and six inches thick, with knobbly bits and spiky things all over it.

"Fucking hell! Is she okay?" I asked. From that day onwards, whenever we played at the Kings Arms in Hawick, we never saw Big Aggie again.

In the sixties, playing in a band was regarded with a certain amount of innocent adulation, no matter how good or bad you were and there were always invites to parties after you had finished your gig. Sometimes, as you were never finished early, you would arrive to find everyone flaked out on the floor and the party well and truly over, but on the whole they were still in full swing when we arrived.

I remember many a time staggering up the garden path in the early hours, heading for bed and meeting my dad as he was heading for work.

"Morning" I'd say.

"Morning" would be the reply, as we passed each other.

A particular party sticks out in my mind during this period. We had been invited to this one in the Morningside area of Edinburgh. For us lads who had been brought up on council estates, this was regarded as a very posh part of town. When we arrived, the party was in full swing and the drink was flowing freely. (We bands never brought drink, as it was an accepted proviso that the hosts should look after their celebrity guests.)

After a few drinks I always get a drunken hunger, so I moved into the kitchen, looking for a snack.

"Make whatever you want", said the hostess. In no time at all I had bacon and eggs on the go, with sausages, tomatoes, and fried bread to finish it off. All the time I was cooking I was being watched by a big black Labrador, who looked at my every move with intense interest.

Having placed my feast on a plate on the table, I turned to the cupboard for some ketchup. On turning around, I was confronted by an empty plate, and a very full Labrador, slinking away to the corner of the kitchen.

"You thieving black bastard, I suppose you'd like a drink as well!" I fumed. I poured the contents of my can of lager into his drinking bowl. He trotted forward and lapped it down in seconds.

"Thirsty are we?" I asked and poured a full can of Guinness into the bowl. That went as fast as the lager. He looked up at me with a satisfied expression on his face.

"Would sir like a cocktail?" I asked, and poured whisky, gin, Bacardi, and any other spirit I could find, into his bowl. He slurped it down like a professional alcoholic. By then even he realised he'd had enough and swayed unsteadily back to his basket in the corner of the room, before slumping unconscious onto his cushion. I made a quick cheese sandwich and rejoined the party.

As the night went on, I can't remember much of what went on as I had filled up on the plentiful supply of booze in the room, but seemingly, I was dancing in the middle of the floor with this sleeping dog wrapped around me and everyone thought it was hilarious.

I was awoken in the morning by the hostess yelling "Bruno, Bruno, oh my god, he's been sick everywhere! And I mean everywhere!"

I forced my bloodshot eyes open and rose from the couch where I had collapsed a few hours earlier and asked, "who's Bruno?"

"It's her dog," said Alan.

I grabbed my jacket and made a swift exit out the back door. (To all animal lovers, I cannot apologise enough).

Chapter Five
A Sea Trip

Hair styles in the sixties changed as fast as the fashions. I remember being the first in town to get an "Afro". This entailed perking your hair, then teasing it out with a specialised "Afro" comb. The result was to look as though you had a giant Brillo pad on your head, the more fluffed up the better. Then came a period when really long hair came into fashion. My "strict but fair" father had suffered the shame of his son with the "Afro" and had reassured all his mates that his son was not a weirdo or a "poof" when I started to grow my flowing mane. (Oh that I could do that now!)

As the weeks went by and the hair grew longer, I could see the look of disapproval on his face. It came to a head one evening as I came into the lounge. The paper he was reading came down from his face and he looked at me earnestly.

"Isn't it time you got that hair cut?" he asked.

"But dad, this is my new image," I said, defending myself.

"I don't care about your bloody image, you look a right scruffy git, so go and get it cut!"

I did the usual teenage thing of muttering and whining to myself and left it at that.

The following week, there was another

confrontation. "I thought I told you to get your hair cut!" He said.

"If I get it cut I'm gonna look stupid!" I said.

"Suit yourself, but if it's not cut by next week, then I'm going to cut it!" He threatened.

"Yeh, sure," came my sarcastic reply.

A week went by and sure enough, I was asked again, "are you going to get that hair cut?"

"Dad", I answered wearily, "I've told you, it's my image."

"Suit yourself" he huffed and the paper came up in front of his face again. I went to bed that night feeling very smug with myself. I had, for the first time, made my father back down.

When I awoke in the morning, it dawned on me that something was not quite right. In front of me, on the pillow, was a pile of hair. I shot bolt upright in bed and put my hand to the back of my head. Ah, there they were, my glorious luxurious locks. But something was different. I felt with my hand to the other side, nothing!

My dear old dad had crept into my room while I was sleeping and had cut half of my locks off up to my neck and left the other half! What was I going to do? I couldn't be seen like this! I couldn't go to my usual hairdressers; I would be a laughing stock.

The only thing to do was go to the local "barbers" and try to get the damage repaired as best as possible. As I slunk into the shop with a hood over my head, the barber looked over and said "you Jock's son?"

I nodded in reply.

"Aye, he said that you would be coming in today." When he'd finished, I looked as though I'd joined the marines. It was a real "short back and sides." As I entered the house I saw him sitting in his chair, with his paper in front of his face. The paper was shaking and you could tell he was laughing silently behind it. (My strict but fair father.)

Around April every year there was an event called the "Glasgow weekend," where a large contingent of the youth of Glasgow headed by ferry to the quiet little island of Arran. For three days, the island would be crammed full of teenagers, hill walking, drinking, dancing, and generally having a whale of a time. Every dancehall would have a band playing and we managed to get booked to play at a place called Whiting Bay. I had managed to get the Monday morning off work, on the promise that I would get back for the afternoon shift.

As soon as you boarded the ferry, the party began. The atmosphere was electric and by the time we docked at Brodick harbor, much drink had been drunk and everyone was in very high spirits. (No pun intended.)

We drove down to Whiting Bay and set up our gear in the hall. Our digs were just next door, so we had plenty of time to get ready. The gig went really well, with a packed hall. There were people who had been out walking all day who came straight into the hall, muddy boots and all, dropped their backpacks, and danced around them. After we had finished, we joined in the party atmosphere. I got in the company of a very pretty girl from Port Glasgow and began looking around for a place where we could be more intimate.

The stage dressing room seemed a likely place, but as I opened the door I heard a "hey! Who's there?"

It was our Jimmy in a state of undress.

"Sorry," I apologised.

"Well, get out and shut the fucking door then!" he stormed.

I retreated back to the hall for more drinks and to think where I could try next. The van was in the yard at the back. Yeah, I thought, quiet, dark, secluded, just the job! I steered my willing partner out to the yard and opened the back doors of the van.

"What the fuck now!" roared a naked Jimmy, who was clearly aroused and ready for action.

"I thought you were still in the dressing room?"

"I was, but Ann here, was worried you would come back in, so will you please fuck off now?" I apologised again and realising the dressing room was now free, took my girl back there, where we spent a very pleasant hour or two together.

I didn't see Jimmy until breakfast time the next morning, and he was in a foul mood.

"You really cocked me up last night," he said. "She wouldn't have any of it after you kept butting in! I'm meeting her today and she has got a car, so…" and with that he led me outside to the main road. "If you are going anywhere today in the van, I'll be heading North," he said, pointing up the road, "and you had better be going South!" he said, darkly.

"No problem", I answered with an apologetic smile.

I was going to stay the day in Whiting Bay with my lady friend, but Jimmy's idea of a van ride seemed too good to miss. A nice scenic trip out and maybe a secluded spot for some amorous seconds sounded good. The rest of the band members were still drunk in bed so I picked up my date and set off.

Arran is a beautiful place and as we drove along the almost deserted roads you could not help but be spellbound by the scenery. We had driven for a half an hour or so and pulled up at the side of the road. There was a small country path leading into a large copse of trees, and we took that, walking arm in arm. As we neared the trees, I saw this pink bottom rising and falling in the thick grass ahead.

"Oh no!" I gasped, "It's him!"

Just then Jimmy's face appeared out of the grass. "I'm gonna kill you ya bastard!" he screamed.

We beat a very hasty retreat. Thankfully for me, there is a proven fact that you cannot run very fast with your trousers around your ankles! Had we both thought it out, Arran is an island, and by one going North, and the other going South, the chances are you are bound to meet in the middle. (But not generally in these circumstances).

I waited back at the digs for Jimmy's return expecting the worst. When he arrived about an hour later, his mood had lightened considerably, and all was forgiven, as he saw the funny side of it all.

"Anyway", he said, she was a crap shag after all the waiting, come on, let's get the rest and go for a pint." Over a few pints, Jimmy came up with an idea for the gig that night. "How about this?" he said. "You all go on stage, and say that you are really sorry, but the singer hasn't turned up, I'll come up to the stage dressed like a tramp, and start heckling you, saying something like, he's rubbish anyway. Then you say, I suppose you think you can do better, and break into our first number. I jump up on the stage, whip all the tramp stuff off, and start singing as normal."

We all agreed that it was a great idea, and

would be something different for the crowd, and went off looking for "tramp stuff" for Jimmy to wear.

That night the hall was packed, and Jimmy got changed into his scruffy gear in the dressing room and slipped outside at the rear of the hall, so as not to be noticed. We all admitted that we had done a good job in finding grotty clothes for him, as he looked like a real down and out.

"See you in a bit" he said, as he left.

The rest of us grabbed our instruments and headed for the stage. The crowd looked up expectantly as we appeared. We looked at each other and passed frantic whispered messages that we had practiced during the day, to make it look as though something had gone wrong. I approached the microphone and announced,

"I'm sorry ladies and gentlemen, but our singer appears to be missing." This was Jimmy's cue to come to the front and start his charade. But nothing happened.

I looked around at the front of the stage. No sign of the little sod anywhere!

"As I was saying, ladies and gentlemen, our singer isn't here, so we will just have to do the best we can, under the circumstances." (This time in a much louder voice).

Still nothing.

I began to break out in a cold sweat, as the crowd were becoming visibly restless.

"Well, get on with it then!" yelled a gangly youth at the front.

Just as we were about to beat a hasty retreat back to the dressing room, there came a voice from the back of the hall.

"I'm here!" yelled Jimmy, "tell these two who I am!" He said. There he was, dressed in his tramp's gear, sandwiched between two burly policemen!

It appeared that, as he was creeping round to the front door of the hall, he had caught the attention of the boys in blue, who, judging by his appearance and suspicious behaviour, decided that he must have been up to no good. His explanation fell on deaf ears, and only after many desperate requests, did they allow him inside. (Under close arrest!)

I beckoned the officers to bring him to the stage and after verifying his story, he was duly relieved of his handcuffs and allowed to begin the show.

All's well that ends well, and the two bobbies stayed for the rest of the gig, even congratulating us on a good night. That night, being the last night, we partied well into the early hours. On awakening in the morning with the mother of all hangovers and an average of three hours sleep over the whole weekend, the realisation that I would have to make it back to work sunk in.

As I staggered in, just in time for the

afternoon shift, I was met by my foreman.

"Oh my god!" He yelled, "just look at you!"

There I stood, face as grey as a corpse, dark glasses hiding bloodshot eyes that were streaming through tiredness and a hairstyle like a burst mattress. He grabbed me and hustled me into the men's toilets.

"Stay there!" he ordered, "I'll come and get you when the shift is over." I sat on the loo seat, shut the door and within seconds, drifted into a blissful sleep.

I can't remember much about getting home, but seemingly, I walked through the door in a zombie state, dropped my case, went upstairs to bed and slept for two days.

Chapter Six
On The Ladder to Fame

As the sixties progressed, "flower power" burst on the scene bringing with it the message of peace and love.

"Make love, not war" was the favourite saying, and most of us tried to do just that to the best of our ability. We all felt really "cool man" wearing our kaftans, flowers, beads, and bells. There were parties called "love-ins," which were nothing more than orgies, where everyone joined in with great enthusiasm, smoking "dope," dancing to sitar music and muttering "peace man." (Of course I didn't do any of that, well, no "dope" anyway!)

Come Monday we would be back at work as normal. I suppose you could call us weekend hippies. There was no AIDS then and the worst thing that could happen to you was catching syphilis or gonorrhoea which could be cured if caught in time. Funnily enough, in all those sex freedom years, I only met one guy who had caught "the clap." (I spoke to him at a safe distance, just in case!)

We had changed management, and our new boss had more influence in the local music scene. He secured a deal for us to support a local top band called "Jury" who were touring at the weekends throughout Scotland.

These guys were a crazy bunch of

lunatics, who played great music and also had an amazing stage show. On most nights, the keyboard player would build up to a crescendo, playing louder and louder, getting more frantic, then stick knives in between the keys to hold them down, as he stood on top of his organ. He would then pull out the knives, and start playing it with his feet! While this was going on, the singer would run around the stage like a madman, kicking speaker cabinets over, which would then explode as they had small charges of powder in them. (The cabinets were fake of course, but the audience were not to know, unfortunately the organ was not and it took a hell of a punishment!)

"Flower Power" was on the wane and "Jury" decided to have a "death of the Flower Power" gig in a local hall. The script was to bring a coffin on to the stage before they began playing. Their roadies solemnly carried it on in a funeral procession, dressed as undertakers, with the "Death March" playing on tape in the background. Inside the coffin, which was decked with beads, bells, and flowers, was Linny, their singer. The idea was for the rest of the band to come on stage, reach their usual crescendo, the Linny would leap up out of the coffin, and the whole band would then attack it with axes, smashing it to pieces. Unfortunately, the band, (rather high on certain substances and liquor) decided to tear the coffin to bits, a little earlier than had been rehearsed. This did not impress a bloodied and lacerated Linny, who was still in the coffin! The crowd were treated to an additional performance of Linny chasing the rest of the band around the stage with his axe flailing, screaming death threats at them.

These exhibitions of stage showmanship had impressed Jimmy over the months we had worked with them and had got him thinking of what we could come up with.

"I know we've got the dance routines," he said "and they go down really well, but I think we need to think of something a bit extra."

"What have you got in mind?" I asked.

"Fire!" he announced dramatically. "That'll get their attention, lots of flames licking over the gear."

"There's no way I'm setting fire to my drums," said Alan.

"No, you've got it all wrong," said Jimmy, "I've got this special stuff from a guy in the pub, and it only burns the fumes, and nothing else," he informed us.

"What's the stuff called?" asked Pete.

"Don't know, it's in this bottle," answered Jimmy. With that he held up an un-labelled bottle full of a clear liquid. I looked at the dubious contents.

"You're not splashing that stuff on my gear!" I informed him. The rest of the band was in complete agreement with me.

"Suit yourselves, but I'm gonna try it out on my mic stand next gig," said Jimmy sulkily.

Friday came and we were halfway through the gig. Jimmy had liberally splashed the "miracle fire" solution all over his mic stand before we started and was still trying to get us to pour some over the rest of the gear, with no success. As the night progressed, it was time for Jimmy's party piece. When we had reached an instrumental break in the number, Jimmy ran off stage and returned with a huge lit candle.

Dramatically, he dropped to his knees, as if in prayer in front of his mic stand, and offered the naked flame to its base. In an instant, the stand ignited and flames licked around it, reaching high into the air.

Jimmy turned to us with a "told you so" look on his face and stood with his arms outstretched, face looking up to the heavens. It was then that the rest of us noticed that things were not quite as they should be, as the paint on his stand began to blister and boil. We tried frantically to get his attention to this problem, but Jimmy in the meantime was oblivious to all this, doing his "holy Jesus" act. With a theatrical flourish, he grabbed the mic stand to continue the song. Instead of the chosen lyrics there came an agonising scream, as the flames shot up his arm.

Luckily there was a fire extinguisher by the side of the stage, and one of our roadies grabbed it and rushed to Jimmy's aid, spraying him from head to foot in a dry mist. The crowd, thinking this was all a part of the show, went berserk. Yes, it certainly was a spectacular stunt, (pity about the second degree burns that it inflicted). Jimmy decided that after his visit to the hospital that we would revert to the safer dance routines!

The band got more popular (without the pyrotechnics) and supported the chart toppers of the time when they appeared in Scotland, The Bee Gee's, Foundations, and the like, but it was becoming apparent that we were almost at the end. We had taken the band about as far as it could go. Jimmy and Soapy were losing interest, and it showed. Pete had left sometime before and had been replaced by Jocky on keyboards which had added a new dimension to the band. But even this wasn't enough for the two of them.

It all came to an end one spring evening, when we had a crisis meeting. Jimmy had decided he wanted to go back to playing rock and roll, whereas Soapy's new wife was not happy at him playing all weekends and most of the week. Pete had just been offered a job with great prospects, but it would mean him travelling away a lot. The bands fate was sealed.

We raised our glasses, wished each other all the best, shook hands and went our separate ways. It's strange to think, that, from being in each other's lives almost every day, I haven't seen Soapy or Pete since that day so many years ago.

Alan phoned me a couple of days later and asked me if I would be interested in forming another band. He had met three guys whose band had just split up at the same time as ours and were keen to start up again. Their band had been quite successful on the local scene as well as ours and we knew them quite well, so Alan, Jocky and I arranged to meet up with them. After only a few minutes, we realised that we had "something", and joined forces.

There was Dougie on vocals, Jake on lead guitar, (who looked like Roy Wood without the beard) and the baby of the band at a tender sixteen years, Archie. (Who later joined The Bay City Rollers on their first hit!) We got down to serious rehearsals, and within a month, the band was sounding good and we were ready to start gigging.

Our manager had stuck by us and agreed to continue to represent us (at the usual fifteen percent of course.) Alan decided to organise a dance in the local community centre for our first gig. It was going to be a big event, with "Jury" headlining. Our band (now called "Tandem") supported second and three lesser known bands, plus a DJ to fill in the rest of the night.

This would take some organising (and money,) but Alan was a great organiser and was in his element. Single handedly he took on the task, and in days, had it set up. Everything was arranged, and the big night came.

We were a little bit apprehensive to say the least, as the cost of staging this event was running at three hundred and fifty pounds. This was a serious amount of money in those days.

Alan had worked it out that we would need four hundred people through the door to break even. There was a little hump-backed bridge on the way to the centre and this gave us a clear view of the people coming to the gig. For the first twenty-five minutes or so, we mentally counted the heads as they filed over the bridge. Our worries were unfounded, as they just kept on coming in their droves. There were over six hundred people at the gig that night, which gave us a very healthy return on our financial gamble. All that was left to do was to give them a great night, and we were up for it.

Our manager approached us and said he had a favour to ask us. He had just taken on this new band, and wanted us to slot them in, in one of the breaks. We agreed to put them on in front of us, as a favour.

Curiosity saw us at the front of the house to watch this "new outfit" do their stuff. They appeared on stage in ice blue suits, with dark glasses over their eyes. In the late sixties it was regarded very old rock and roll and out of date. The jeering of the crowd left the poor guys in no doubt about it. Worse was to follow when they began playing. They were bloody awful! I thanked God that they were only doing fifteen minutes. I marched up to our boss and demanded, "Tam, where the fuck did you dig up this load of shite from? They are absolutely the worst load of crap I've ever heard!"

He looked at me and said, "they are gonna be big someday!"

"I think you have been at the whisky!" I replied, (knowing that he didn't drink.) "What's this pile of crap called anyway?" I asked.

"The Bay City Rollers," he answered.

The period that followed that event became quite a roller coaster ride in my life. (No "roller" pun intended.) We had attracted quite a large following in Edinburgh and to our surprise, so had the "Rollers." We had now become the two most popular bands around. The difference between our two bands were, although we would play up to our female support, we always kept a few tunes for the guys to have a slow dance at the end and give them a chance to get a girl.

The "Rollers" on the other hand would play strictly for the girls only and stick to "bubble gum" music as it was sarcastically known.

Tam Paton, our manager, had read Brian Epstein's book (the Beatles manager) from cover to cover, and decided he would mould our two bands in the same way. That meant no girls, no drinking to excess and always to be seen out together at all times, showing what best buddies we were.

The "Rollers" followed these instructions to the letter, whereas we tended to bend the rules just a little bit. A prime example of this "bending" of the rules was by me. I had met this girl and had become quite serious about her. A rare occasion happened when Tam had slipped up and we had a night free of rehearsals or meetings. He had instructed us to have a quiet night in and think up some ideas for new numbers. I seized my chance and devised a plan to spend that evening with my girl. I dressed up in "naff" clothes, wore dark glasses, and combed my hair flat across my brow to disguise myself, in case any of our fans recognised me.

I caught the bus to Musselburgh and instead of taking the local transport to Whitecraig, where my girl lived, I took a bus to the main depot in the centre of Edinburgh. From there I caught a bus to Bonnyrigg, a town near Whitecraig, then finally, a short trip to her house. A journey which should have taken fifteen minutes to complete, had taken over an hour and a half, but I felt it was worth it.

I was feeling pretty pleased with myself as I opened the gate to the path to her house, when a car I recognised pulled up slowly beside me. My heart sank, it was Tam! The window wound down. "Get in the car," he barked.

"But I'm just visiting my mate!" I said lamely.

"No you're not", he said "you're here to see your bird." I slumped down in the seat of the car and asked him how he possibly could have known about it.

"You can't keep any secrets from me, girls love to talk, and yours is no different." "Listen," he said earnestly, "how do you think you can keep your fans interested in you, if they know you have a girlfriend?" He went on to explain, that to keep our fans, we all had to appear to be available and therefore let them think they all had a chance to be with us. I had to admit that his logic was pretty sound and I could see where it could lead, but it did nothing for my love life at the time.

As I said before, our two bands had captured all the top billings in the area, and our followings grew by the week but even this didn't do it for Jocky and he decided to call it a day and we reverted to a five-piece outfit. It became the "norm" to pack the dance halls out wherever we played, and the girls would go mad, screaming and jumping onto the stage, trying to get to us. It could get quite rough sometimes, with the fans that got to us ripping the shirts off our backs as a "memento" (They would grab other things as well and providing they weren't too rough, it could be quite a pleasant experience.)

This happened so often that we had an

account with the local top boutique Top Man, supplying us with at least five shirts and two pairs of trousers every week. It cost us a fortune, but we accepted the fact that it was a small price to pay for the publicity in the local press it was creating. Our roadies on the other hand, would grumble that they had enough to do without having to haul girls off us on the stage and toss them back into the crowd. We would have a constant change of road crew as the work was hard and they were paid little for doing it.

As we were paid not much more (if anything) after expenses, we understood their plight, but couldn't do much more for them, say a meal now and then after the gig. Those who joined thinking they would meet lots of women, soon found out that there was no time, as they were always either setting up or stripping down the equipment, but to me they will always be the unsung heroes.

Tam was growing increasingly exasperated with us, as we were bending the rules a little too much for his liking. He was constantly telling us that we should act more like the "Rollers," and stick to his ideas, but we thought we knew better.

The crunch came when a big gig came up for us both. We were to play in a village called Rosewell for the convent nun's charity there. Jimmy Saville's mother had been helped by the nuns there and he had decided to appear there to raise funds for them as a show of appreciation. To play in front of the top DJ in the land at the time, was our chance to be recognised and maybe get signed up for a record deal if we impressed him enough.

Both bands were buzzing and looking forward eagerly to showing Mr Saville what we could do. With the combined fans of the two bands, it was guaranteed to be a sell-out electric atmosphere. I have to say, that on the musical side of the scale, we were streets ahead of the "Rollers", and our fans tended to be noisier and more enthusiastic. With that knowledge inside us we had no qualms that Jimmy would be well impressed with us. The night before the gig something happened, that to this day, I have still to find out the reason for the events that followed.

Tam phoned us to say that the gig was cancelled, but he had managed to re-book us in the border town of Melrose. We were bitterly disappointed and were feeling pretty low about it. He was quick to reassure us that there would be another time when we could show Mr Saville what we were made of, but that didn't help at the time. The following evening saw five dejected guys and their road crew set off for Melrose in very low spirits indeed. On arrival we were greeted by the organiser, who was so-so grateful, and could not thank us enough for doing this charity gig for the local paraplegic society. (News to us!)

On entering the hall we saw that it was full of people in wheelchairs.

"This is a dance isn't it?" I asked.

"Oh yes", replied the man in charge, "don't you worry, they'll be dancing alright." As the night wore on, they certainly showed the more able people how to strut their stuff, as they spun and gyrated around the dance floor. As the dance ended, we were greeted with wild applause, which made us feel it had been all worthwhile.

"Thank you very much", I said, "we've often had a standing ovation before, but this is the first time we've had a sitting one!" This was taken in the light-hearted way it was given and they cheered even louder. As we packed our gear away we felt that it wasn't such a bad night after all.

The following day we found out the gig with Jimmy Saville hadn't been cancelled after all. He had seen the "Rollers" with their fans screaming for them and had been suitably impressed. Our fans had not been told that we would not be there, and somehow Tam had managed to turn them away from the gig. How he did this without causing uproar is still a mystery to me. As for the "Rollers" the rest is history. For the first time, but not the last, we learned never to trust managers and agents as far as you could throw them.

Our relationship with Tam deteriorated after that. He kept promising that when the "Rollers" were "big" he could concentrate on us, but his time, more and more, were taken up with them. My relationship with my girl had survived, and it had reached the commitment stage, so much so, that Tam gave me an ultimatum. It was the band or the girl. They say love is blind and I suppose they could be right, because I decided to leave and make a life with her. So ended my chapter as an aspiring pop star. (Nearly famous!)

Chapter Seven
Howdy Partners

The next few months were spent with my now fiancé just leading a normal life, working and going out at the weekends, meeting friends for a drink, the usual things. Having worked so hard with "Tandem" to make the grade, it was nice to have a break, but it wasn't long before I began to get the urge to start up again.

I became friends with my fiancé's friend's boyfriend and found out that he played guitar. He knew a guy who played drums, and suggested we team up and form a trio. Country and Western music was riding high (excuse the pun) at the time in the late sixties and we concentrated on that as there were plenty of outlets for it, and the money was good.

With Al on guitar, Reg on drums, and myself Brick on bass, we called ourselves "The Bar-T." (Brick, Al, Reg trio, get it!) We soon had a full diary for the coming year. To give it a little authenticity we dressed in black, with red bandanas around our necks, but drew the line at wearing cowboy hats. There were plenty of those hats around when we played at a few Country and Western society gigs. They would all dress up in their finest cowboy and cowgirl clothes, with the guys having guns strapped around their waists. They would have "shoot-outs" to find the fastest draw and all have western names. (Personally, I think if they had used real bullets instead of blanks, it would have been more interesting.)

It was a little strange to be talking to "The Colorado Kid" only to find out he was a milkman from Tranent in real life. To be fair to them, it was their passion, and they lived the dream to the hilt.

The beginning of the seventies saw us tiring of the Country and Western scene and we began to incorporate a few popular numbers into our repertoire. Not to take anything away from country songs, but as one guy said to us, to write the ultimate western song, you would sing about a granny in a wheelchair going over a cliff, with a cute little dog in her lap, landing on top of an orphan, killing all three. Very sad, but very sellable.

We were approached by the landlord of the "Coach House" in Loanhead, which was a mining village about six miles from Musselburgh. He wanted us to be the resident band there on Fridays and Saturdays, but insisted on no country songs. This made our minds up and we decided to take him up on his offer and put Country and Western out to graze. (Excuse another pun!).

Having never been in a residency before, we found it strange to leave our gear there permanently and only have to turn up about ten minutes before we had to play. It certainly made life a lot easier. The down side (there always is one) was that you knew that most of every weekend would be taken up and because it was mostly the same people turning up, we had to learn new numbers on a regular basis.

We settled into the routine and everything became pretty much predictable, apart from one very memorable instance. The boss approached us one night and said he had a favour to ask us. He had a friend who was visiting him from London where he worked as a singer in the clubs. He wondered if his friend could do a couple of numbers with us.

"We don't read music, and we haven't had any experience of backing singers," I said.

"That's no problem" he answered, "he's only doing the easy stuff, you'll follow him no bother."

"What stuff does he do?" asked Reg.

"Elvis Presley," replied the boss.

"Ok, we'll I've it a bash," said Reg.

We began playing and the hall began to fill up with the usual Friday night crowd. The three of us were beginning to get a bit nervous about the guest artiste, as he hadn't even been in touch with us to tell us what songs he would be singing.

At ten o' clock on the dot he strode in, making a grand entrance, dressed in the full "Elvis" regalia, with the jumpsuit covered in sequins, the dark glasses, the cape, the complete package. Unannounced, he jumped up onto the stage.

"Just follow me", he whispered as he grabbed the microphone. "Good evening ladies and gentlemen," he announced in a very bad American accent and even worse "Elvis" drawl. "Welcome to my show!"

Reg, Ally and I looked at each other. What was all this "my show" crap!

"Here's a little number I'm sure you'll recognise," and with that he launched into his act. Not only had he forgotten to tell us what he was singing, but he hadn't told us the key either. You can imagine the utter chaos that followed, with two guitarists flapping up and down the fret boards, trying to find the right notes, and a drummer frantically trying to pick out the tempo through all this mayhem.

The shambles lasted for about ten seconds before "Elvis" called a halt.

"Whoa, whoa", he cried, "it seems my band ain't ready for the King just yet," he joked. (His band!)

Ally leaned over to him. "What fucking song are you supposed to be singing?" he hissed. "Suspicious Minds" came the answer.

"And what fucking key would that be in?" added Ally, dryly.

"It's in "C" replied our superstar.

"Right, now we've got that cleared up, we can start again" said Ally, in none too good a humour.

With this information we kicked off again, and things were going really well until the "King" began to sing. He was so off-key, that if he had been a dog you would have shot him out of mercy. His timing was no better, as every time we caught up with him, he would either slow down, or speed up, which would throw us off the tempo again. We somehow managed to limp through the number and finish roughly together. It was greeted with a small ripple of applause. (Most of it out of sympathy in my view.)

"Thank you, thank you very much," drawled our hero, oblivious to the lack of response from the audience.

"I must apologise ladies and gentlemen, but I'm not used to working with amateurs like these guys," he said, pointing at us.

This was too much for Reg, who had a short fuse to his temper at the best of times. He shot up from his drums, scattering them everywhere, walked up to the front of the stage, grabbed the microphone from our "artiste" and said, "and we're not used to working with shite!"

With that he jumped off the stage and strode up to the bar and ordered himself a beer. This was greeted with wild applause and laughter from the crowd. With his feelings hurt and his feathers well and truly ruffled our

"Elvis," in one of his shortest performances ever, left the building.

Even though we would try and change the numbers in our routine as often as possible, we were becoming bored with life at the "Coach House." I ran into an old friend called Jimmy. He was only twenty-two years old, but he was already making a name for himself as a very funny comedian on the local cabaret circuit. He was, and still is, a very colourful character.

At the tender age of fourteen he decided to start his own "pirate" radio station from his bedroom. Every night he would raise his transmitter mast in his back garden and go on the air for an hour. After his broadcast he would sign off, lower his mast, go back to his bedroom, and finish his homework for school the following morning. He had a transmitting radius of about twenty-five miles and was becoming so popular that he was catching the attention of the broadcasting authorities. They spent many fruitless weeks trying to track him down using tracker vans and when they eventually caught him and found out that they had been given the run-around by a fourteen-year old schoolboy, they decided not to press charges and hushed the whole thing up to hide their embarrassment.

Whilst chatting with Jimmy he came up with the suggestion that we could start a comedy band. Although he was doing really well on his own, he wanted to try something a little different. He had this idea in his head what the format would be. A band, a comedian and a main singer. Put them all together and that would be your comedy band package for the cabaret circuit. He was also a very good impressionist, and could take off Tommy Cooper, Norman Wisdom, and the like. Jimmy was working alongside a guy called Dougie, who could sing and impersonate Tom Jones, Roy Orbison, and Elvis.

"Honest Brick, he looks just like Tom Jones, the hair, the build, the looks, everything," said Jimmy. (To the modern-day reader, all these characters seem like "old hat," but in the early seventies they were at their most popular.)

"It could really work", he continued, "Besides, have you seen any other Scottish comedy bands doing the rounds? We could be the first."

I had to admit that I hadn't.

"I'll talk to the lads and see what they say," I promised. "We're at the Coach House, come and see us there," I said.

Jimmy agreed to visit us shortly and we left it at that.

At the weekend, I spoke to the others about the idea, and they were both keen to give it a try. Weeks went by with no sign of Jimmy and we assumed that he had had second thoughts about it. One Saturday morning while walking down Musselburgh's Main Street, I bumped into him again.

"Have you spoken to the lads yet?" he asked.

"Christ Jimmy that was ages ago," I answered.

"I know, I know, but I'm still keen to give it a try, and Dougie is raring to go as well." He promised to come to the "Coach House" that evening and bring Dougie with him. To my surprise, they turned up that night and sat at the front, watching the band. At the end of the night Jimmy introduced us to Dougie. He wasn't wrong about the similarity to Tom Jones. He could have passed as his double!

"How about we get together one night and see how it goes?" suggested Jimmy. I told him we could get the "Coach House" any night of the week if we wanted it.

"How about Wednesday night?" offered Jimmy. All of us agreed. "See you Wednesday then," called Jimmy from the doorway.

That meeting was to change all our lives and open the door to the crazy world of cabaret for the next two decades.

Chapter Eight
Life is a cabaret old chum

Wednesday night came and we cautiously got down to the work at hand.

"I suppose you'll want to hear our Dougie do his stuff right away," said Jimmy.

"Yeh, what you gonna sing Doug?" asked Reg.

"It's not unusual," offered Dougie, "but I have to warn you, I don't read music," he apologised.

"No worries there, neither the fuck does us," laughed Reg.

We let Dougie sing a few bars of the song and picked up his key. He was brilliant. If you closed your eyes you would swear it was Tom Jones singing.

"Wow! We're on a winner there Dougie," I said. He had only sung in public at parties before, but with a little bit of grooming he was going to be great. Jimmy went through a few of his comedy routines and impressions and had us in stitches. We worked with Dougie on a few more of his numbers and then sat down to work out a format for our cabaret show.

The format was to be the band starting the show with a couple of numbers, then introduce Dougie as Tom Jones, followed by Jimmy, who would come on as Norman Wisdom, falling all over the place, before launching into a joke-telling routine.

This would give Dougie time to change into his Roy Orbison props. After that take-off, Jimmy would appear as Tommy Cooper and so on. Any gaps in the show, or time needed for major dress changes would be filled with the band's music.

In no time and with hard work, our show was ready to go. To pay the boss for the use of the hall, we said we would stage our very first show on a Wednesday night. Surprisingly, the place was packed that night, with curious regulars and strangers coming to see this new comedy band. They all loved it. The reception we received was way beyond our wildest expectations. They kept roaring for more, long after we had finished.

With that show boosting our confidence we started to look for an agent who would get us on the cabaret circuit. This, we thought would only be a formality, but as we were soon to learn, it was like hitting your head against a brick wall. Every agent we tried would ask the same question. They would ask us where they could come and see us, if they could spare the time. We would answer that we didn't have any venues as yet and that was why we were phoning them. The reply from all of them was the same. They couldn't book us without seeing us. (A very catch-22 situation.)

The band continued to play at the "Coach

House" at the weekends and sometimes Jimmy would come to tell us he had found another agent who might be interested in us, but it never materialised. (He admitted later that he just made those stories up to give us hope and keep us going.) We would rehearse the act every fortnight or so to add things and keep it in our minds, but it was becoming clear that it was a lost cause, or so we thought.

The "Coach House" was becoming a chore to do by this time and Reg decided he had had enough. Ally and I felt much the same way, so we handed our notice in to the boss. He said he was sad to see us go, but as there was no binding contract, he couldn't keep us there.

As has happened throughout my musical career, just when I thought I'd played my last, something else would turn up. Jimmy phoned me to say he had found an agent willing to take a chance on us.

"Who is this guy?" I asked warily.

"He only does it part-time", said Jimmy, "and he only has a few clubs on his books, but it's a start."

I contacted Ally, who, like myself, was very sceptical. "This is not another one of Jimmy's would-be agents is it?" he said.

"No, this is a definite," I answered.

Reg made it clear that he was not interested and was still going to leave. Jimmy and Dougie came over to see us with the details of our first gig.

"It's in two weeks in Ayrshire," said Jimmy.

"Ayrshire! That's fucking miles away!" I said.

"I know, but the agent fella wanted to make sure that if we died on our arses it would be far enough away from him to get any bother, and anyway it's the first time he has had an act in the club," said Jimmy.

"Well, we've got a little problem, Reg's leaving." I said.

Reg turned to Jimmy. "Sorry mate, but I don't think I'm cut out for this cabaret stuff."

"A little bit of notice would have come in handy," Jimmy replied icily. " I run around like a headless chicken to get us started and now you say you are fucking leaving!" he moaned.

Reg leapt up from his chair. "Get fucked!" he stormed, and stomped out the door, nearly taking it off its hinges as he slammed it shut behind him.

"And fuck you too!" yelled Jimmy after him. He paused for a moment and said, "that could have gone a bit better couldn't it?"

"Just a bit", I answered. "But we are now left with the problem of having no drummer, and a gig in two weeks."

Just then a thought came to me. I'd heard that "Tandem" had broken up and if that was the case, then Alan would be available.

"I think I might have someone for the job," I said. I picked up the phone and dialled his number. "Alan," I said.

"Yeh," he answered.

"Get your arse round to my house double quick, I've got a job for you," I demanded. He was there in five minutes, asking what was going on.

"We're starting a comedy cabaret band, are you interested?" I asked him.

"Sounds different, Yeh, count me in," he said.

"Good, our first gig is in two weeks, so let's get down to it."

"Two weeks! That's a bit short notice, isn't it?"

"It's more than the three days you gave me when I started with the "In-Sense," I laughed.

"Point taken", he replied.

True to form, our Alan was ready well within the time set for our first cabaret gig. We arrived at the club and were surprised to see how big it was inside, considering how small the village was. (Sorry but the name escapes me.)

To make us welcome, the committee took great pleasure in telling us how difficult the crowd were to please. (This would be standard throughout my cabaret career in many different clubs and countries.) Social committees are a strange breed of human being. During the day, they work at their normal jobs, i.e. bus drivers, joiners, etc, but at night they become club secretary, entertainments official and the like.

What has always amazed me, is that they generally have had no training or experience in any of the jobs given them by the clubs and for most part, are never paid for their labours. I can only presume, by past encounters, that the power of wearing the committee badge and "lording it" over all and sundry was payment enough.

"We've had some right shite here lately," informed our entertainments overseer, "so you'd better be good or they won't waste time in telling you," he said, nodding towards the crowd.

"We're a bit nervous," Jimmy replied. "You see, this is our very first performance in cabaret."

"Christ on a stick! That's just fucking marvelous, ain't it?" He thundered. "I can see this is gonna be one for the "hook."

Having put us at ease with his words of encouragement, our mentor headed for the door of the dressing room.

"You're on in twenty minutes after the bingo and don't be swearing on stage, they don't like that," was his parting comment.

"Right you fucking are," replied Jimmy, his attempt at satire falling on deaf ears.

It never fails to amaze me, the change in attitude of people (and committees) when you do a good show and that first show was a really, really good show. As the show went on, from being greeted with hostile stares, and suspicious looks, we were suddenly looked upon with smiles, admiring glances, and, truth be known, a little awe.

Our patron from the dressing room wasted no time in telling everyone how much of a risk he had taken to book this unknown commodity and that he had gone with his gut feeling about us. With much backslapping, and handshaking at the end of the show, he whisked us off to the bar for a drink.

"When can we book you guys again?" he asked.

"You'd better get in touch with our agent," said Jimmy importantly.

"I'll be on the phone first thing Monday morning!" He promised. We drove the long journey home feeling very pleased with ourselves.

The phone call to the agent must have been a glowing report, because, that Monday evening, he was on the phone to Jimmy giving us bookings for the following three Saturdays.

The other bookings went as well as the first and we were booked for six more. Up to this point we had never met the guy, but with all the great reports he had coming back from the clubs we had played, it was only a matter of time before we did. Halfway between our batches of six bookings, he said he was coming to see us. He turned up in a suit, carrying a briefcase, looking every inch the agent.

After the show, with the crowd going wild (as usual) he sat us down and said he wanted to manage us.

"What's the difference between management and agency?" Enquired Jimmy.

"About ten percent more out of our wages," replied Alan dryly.

"No, no, it's not like that at all," promised Mike, our manager to be. "I'll be promoting you, doing all the publicity, making sure you will be my top priority for bookings, because I think that you've got something special there."

We had a quick conference between ourselves and were all of the same opinion that we had nothing to lose and after all, as he had been the only person to take us on, deserved the chance to be in sole charge of our future. In the coming months, this worked out really well for both parties as he was able to promote us to other agencies and sell his other acts to the clubs we had played.

We were constantly updating the act and improving it as we gained more experience. Jimmy and I struck up a "funny man straight man" partnership. It just came naturally as Jimmy never did the same routine twice. He was always throwing in extra gags, or changing the routine and as I was the link man for all the changes, he used me as the butt for his jokes. It worked out really well as I could play the "bad guy" in some of the sketches. I played it so well in fact, that on several occasions I would be accosted after the show by irate punters telling me to leave that poor guy (Jimmy) alone.

Mike had called a photo-shoot a few weeks earlier and with our new stage suits, had been told to sit there, stand here, look this way, look that way, by the photographer. We had heard nothing since and frankly had been so busy that we had forgotten about it.

"Come into the office" Mike told us over the phone, "I've something to show you."

We trooped in and there on his desk was a pile of photographs with our ugly mugs on them, with the title of "The Mimics, Scotland's Top Comedy Band" emblazoned underneath.

It all looked very grand and professional and we were really pleased with the finished article.

"No more than you guys deserve, because you are the top!" Stated Mike.

Work was piling in, and we had to revise our transport situation. Up to that point we had been using three cars and my old minivan to shift our gear and props about. (It's amazing how much stuff you can cram into a minivan.) Mike decided we needed a proper band vehicle and set me the task of finding one. My uncle was in the used car business, so I thought that being family, he would give me a good deal.

He sold me an "Atlas" van for sixty pounds. It'd had a new paint job done on it and it sounded OK to my inexperienced ears. He told me I was getting it cheap as I was family and not to thank him. If you have ever had the misfortune to drive one of those, you would know that they were never in the same class as the Ford Transit (not even close!) The front end sat well down. So much so that you would think it had the two front tyres punctured. Behind the driver's cab, the bodywork rose up to give it a "hunchback" look. The two front seats were separated by the engine cowling in the middle which gave off enough heat to boil an egg. (Great in winter, not so much in the summer months!)

The designer's master stroke had to be the gear stick. It was situated at the very back of the cowling. First, second, and third gears were attainable with difficulty, but fourth gear was virtually impossible unless you tore your arm out of its socket or turned around one hundred and eighty degrees to engage it. As for reverse, I don't think The Great Houdini could have managed it alone, but I thought, for sixty pounds, we could put up with these little problems.

That night we had a gig in Haddington, which was about fifteen miles away. We set off in our new "band wagon" and had only gone about three miles, when steam began pouring out of the engine.

"Fan belts snapped" said Ally, after a quick inspection, "anyone got a pair of tights?" he asked. Dougie's girlfriend duly obliged and Ally tied them around the pulley wheels. Off we set again with the temporary repair holding up well. Within five minutes there was a clattering sound from underneath.

"Fucking exhaust's fell off now," informed Ally, who was getting dirtier by the minute. There followed a period of much banging and cursing from below the van before a filthy Ally informed us that, that was the best he could do under the circumstances. The now exhaustless engine started up with an almighty roar that would have shattered a decibel meter a mile away. It was so noisy, that even when we shouted directly into each other's ears, you couldn't be heard.

We hadn't gone two miles before we attracted the attention of the boys in blue.

"Good evening Sirs" the officer said in a tired voice, "do you realise you have a defective exhaust?" He looked in the cab and saw Ally's grimy face.

"Oh, I see you do," he said. "Well, you can't drive on the public highway with a vehicle in that state, you're going to have to get it towed home."

I looked at him pleadingly, "but we've got

a gig in Haddington, and we're late as it is." Just then, the other policeman came to the cab window.

"Are you that comedy lot from Musselburgh?" he asked.

"Yes!"

"Saw you in Whitecraig club, you're really good." He motioned his partner to join him at the back of the van and there followed a whispered discussion between them for a few moments.

"Right," he said, as he rejoined us, "we'll let you carry on, but if you get stopped again, we never saw you, so take it easy on the throttle, and try to keep the noise down." We thanked him and carried on our way.

On arriving at the club we were met by a very angry committee who had just about given up on us. We explained what had happened, and one look at Ally's filthy appearance proved that we weren't telling lies. The gear was set up in record time and the show started forty minutes later than billed. The crowd, whom had been noisy and restless because of the delay, soon warmed to us and we received a great reception at the end of the show.

"Lads, that was brilliant," said one of our hosts "but we're going to have to dock you thirty quid off the fee because we had to miss out three games of bingo."

Bingo! Sigh, the curse of the cabaret

artiste. Everything in club land must revolve around it. Admittedly, it was a major source of income for the clubs, but in most of these places it took over and became the priority. With our pockets a little lighter than they should have been we set off for home. On the outskirts of the town we had a puncture.

"Where's the spare wheel in this heap of crap?" Asked Ally.

"Ah, it's in the back, behind the gear," I answered apologetically. He gave me a withering look.

"Does this fucking uncle of yours hold a grudge against you?" he asked. It took fifteen minutes to empty out the van and get the wheel, another fifteen were spent putting it all back in, and finally we were on our way once again. "Take this crap heap back to that uncle of yours, and get our money back", ordered Ally. The next day I took the van back to my uncle and because I was family, he gave me forty pounds for it. (I wondered which family he meant). I didn't dare tell the band, especially Ally, that I'd lost twenty pounds on the deal, so I put the difference in the kitty out of my own pocket. Having learnt my lesson, (and never to trust close relatives ever again) I went to Mike and borrowed enough money to buy a decent Transit van.

About this time there was a show on TV called "Opportunity Knocks" which was hosted by a Canadian called Hughie Green. It was the most popular Saturday night TV show at that time. Hughie would introduce a few unknown acts on his show and at the end, the studio audience would vote for the one they liked best.

There would also be a vote from the TV viewers and the best act (or most popular) would be invited back the following week. That act could be invited back week after week, making them household names and "stars" in the process.

To discover these acts, Mr Green would travel all over Britain, holding auditions in all the major towns. Mike had decided to try us for the show when the auditions came to Carlisle. We arrived there to find hundreds of people milling around, waiting to be seen. There were dancers, singers, bands, magicians, all kinds of different entertainers. You can imagine that this was not like the X Factor which is on our screens today which is much more limited. The hopefuls back then would have all their equipment with them. Drums, guitars, flaming hoops etc.

As you can imagine. The scene was chaotic. As we waited our turn, a frantic magician was desperately trying to catch one of his doves which was flying up and down the auditorium, crapping on everyone below.

Our turn finally came and we were given fifteen minutes to set-up our gear and be ready to play. The floor manager told us in no uncertain terms that if we missed our deadline, we would be passed over for the next act, which was already waiting and ready to go. It's amazing what you can do when blind panic takes over. Fifteen minutes later, and we were set up and ready to go.

Mr Green and his two producers came to a halt in front of us and beckoned us to begin. We had condensed a five-minute routine, all prepared just for him. When we had finished, Hughie and his TV advisors went into a huddle and talked earnestly for a minute or so.

"That was great guys," he said. "I think it's safe to say you'll be on the show!" We jumped around screaming and yelling like idiots. We were going to be on the telly!

Details were passed to the girl in charge of the technical side, with the assurance that Mr Green's office would be in touch within the week. We were brought down to earth almost immediately by a stagehand who ordered us to "get your fucking shit out of the way for the next act."

Mike wasted no time in telling everybody in the business about our forthcoming TV appearance. A couple of days later, I noticed something strange as I walked through the factory gates into work. The security guard was smiling at me. I thought it was weird, as I'd never seen that miserable bastard do that before. As I went to clock-in, people were saying "hi!" and winking at me. I carried on to my work area and all my workmates suddenly stood and began clapping.

"What's going on?" I asked.

"Haven't you seen the morning paper?" Asked a girl I worked alongside.

"No, why?" I asked again.

"You're in it!" She squealed.

I grabbed the paper from her hand, and there it was. Middle page, full colour spread photo, in the top national Scottish newspaper. The story underneath was all about Hughie Green finding this new talent and how he thought that we were sure to be big.

I was so high with excitement that the boss let me have the day off to calm down. I must have bought a dozen copies, just to show anybody unfortunate enough to be near me that day.

I drove to my father's workplace armed with a copy. "Have you seen the paper?" I asked.

He frowned at me. "What are you doing off work?" He asked me.

"The boss gave me the day off. Have you seen the paper?" I repeated.

"Aye. I've seen it."

"Well, what do you think?" I persisted.

"It certainly is a grand bit of publicity for you lads," he said. "But don't forget, tomorrow morning some hairy-arsed shepherd in Stornoway will be wiping his bum with your face!" (Sigh. My strict but fair father.)

Mr Green had organized us to play on his travelling stage show and a gig was set up to perform in Motherwell. We were taking the place of Bobby Crush, a pianist who had won fame on the TV show. We felt very important and "special" on hearing this news. Mike had insisted we rehearse over and over again for our appearance, but with all the normal shows, and knowing our act inside out, or so we thought, we reckoned we could carry it off with ease. And anyway, we were enjoying all the attention we were getting.

As we set up for the Motherwell show, Mr Green came over to wish us well and to tell us that our TV appearance was to be very soon. Life has a way of bringing you back down to earth with a bang, and it certainly did that to us on that night.

Having been given a glowing introduction by Mr Green, proclaiming that we were the next best thing to come out of Scotland, we kicked off into our routine. In the middle of it, for some inexplicable reason, some of the cues got crossed and it ended up a shambles. We managed to recover slightly, but it must have appeared very amateurish.

We never saw or heard from Hughie Green again. Mike, who had watched the whole sad thing, was absolutely furious with us. It made us realise that fame and fortune does not come without hard work. A hard lesson learned too late to save our TV career at the time.

Despite this set-back, our popularity increased by the week, as we travelled up and down the country. In those days it was common to have cabaret shows on almost every evening in the clubs, and we were doing seven evening shows and a Sunday matinee show as well. All this, and holding down a full-time job as well, was extremely tiring, but the money helped. It was too much for Dougie though, and he told us he would be leaving. It was a major blow to us because his special talents made us think he would be impossible to replace. Ally made it a double whammy with the news that he was emigrating to South Africa.

Once again, I found myself in the position of having to start again from almost scratch. Mike had been scouring club land to find replacements and had found two guys whom he said could replace Dougie. They were a comedy impressionist duo who were doing well, but realised that by joining us, they could go much farther. One played keyboards, so that would add a new musical dimension to the band. An old friend of mine called Charlie, who played excellent guitar, also joined, making us a six-piece unit.

There was a talent contest run by the top Edinburgh newspaper which was called "Search for a Star." They held the event every year throughout central Scotland, and around two thousand hopefuls, from the most inexperienced to the top line professionals entered. Mike had entered us and I was a bit sceptical, because, depending on the judges, we could be beaten by a three-year old tap dancer, or a dog that could jump through hoops in time to music. (The old scenario, never work with kids or animals!)

Mike assured us that because of our widespread popularity, we would only be called in at the later stages. We entered the contest in the last two hundred and won all our heats to reach the grand final.

The final was being staged in the Mecca theatre in Edinburgh in front of a sell-out two thousand crowd. In total there were ten acts in contention for the prizes on offer. The first prize was a cruise on the P and O flagship "The Canberra," a week performing at the "Batley Variety Theatre," a gallon of whisky from one of the sponsors (after all, it was in Scotland,) three thousand pounds in cash and free publicity in the local press. In addition to this, it was going to be pre-recorded by the local radio station and broadcast later in the week following.

All the acts were of a high standard as you would expect and most of us knew each other from the entertainment circuit. We all wished each other well for the coming evening. At the end of the contest, when we had all done our best, the waiting for the results began.

This has been perfected over the years, and in recent TV programmes, has been milked to the utmost. This is a traumatic time for the artiste when the stakes are so high in any competition, and to have to wait for that drawn out gap in the results is a torture we don't really need, but I suppose its good television.

A rumour was going around backstage that the winner would either be a solo or duo act due to the expense of the trip on "The Canberra." As a six-piece, we had no illusions of our chances and had resigned ourselves to hoping to win one of the three remaining places. With the judging completed, we were all lined up on stage for the results.

Fourth place was announced, going to a solo act. Then came third place, won by a four-piece band. Second place went to a male singer, and we looked crestfallen at each other.

"And now ladies and gentlemen! The winner of Search For A Star nineteen seventy five is... and God help "The Canberra" when these maniacs get on board... The Mimics!"

We looked at each other in disbelief, jaws open, we'd won! There followed much camera flashing, and oversized cheques being passed over and back-slapping and handshaking, but we hadn't taken it all in and were in a daze.

Only when the commotion had died down an hour or so later did we have a chance to let it sink in, in the privacy of our dressing room. We all just stared at each other, with silly grins on our faces, shaking our heads in disbelief.

Chapter Nine
Life on the Ocean Waves

The next few months were hectic, with guest appearances here and there, whilst still performing eight shows a week. The money improved noticeably and more prestigious bookings came our way. The down side was that my marriage was beginning to suffer because of it.

I had two sons by this time and what with the cabaret commitments and still holding down a full-time job, I never had enough time to spend with them. I had this idea in my head that if we could make it to the top I could give it two years and then settle down with enough money to live comfortably from then on.

One occasion springs to mind. I returned home one evening at a rare early time to find my youngest son Bryan tottering around the house.

"He's walking!" I cried.

"He's been walking for three weeks!" My wife replied acidly.

Nineteen seventy-five went and seventy-six was brought in with us playing a late night cabaret in Glasgow. Our social life was now non-existent, and even special occasions in our private lives (birthdays etc.) were sacrificed.

Bobby and Lee, the duo who had joined up, lived near Bathgate, which was twenty-five miles from us, so even after the gigs, more time was spent travelling to drop them off at home.

The cruise on The Canberra was arranged for July of that year and we were excitedly looking forward to it as we would be performing on board, as well as being on the list as passengers. I thought this would be a great opportunity to patch things up with my wife. One month before we were due to sail a bombshell was dropped on us. Only the band had tickets to sail. No provision had been made for wives and girlfriends. Even Mike, our manager, was not included. Jimmy and Alan had decided to pay for their wives passage, but the rest of us couldn't really afford it at that time. When I told my wife the news this only soured our relationship even farther. As I was under contract, there was no way out of it. I would have to go on the cruise, or it would affect everyone concerned.

As we drove down to Southampton to catch the ship I sat with mixed emotions. On one hand there was excitement at the thought of a Mediterranean cruise in front of me and on the other was my marriage, which was now going into free fall. On arriving at the docks I selfishly put my marital problems to one side and was caught up in the excitement of this new adventure.

The Canberra was a beautiful ship. Huge, gleaming, white and majestic as she lay moored at her dock.

"Are you crew?" asked one of the ships officers, as we loaded our equipment into one of the bays.

"Yes" I replied, "we're the Mimics." He looked down his list and shook his head.

"You're not on here", he informed us.

"Well, we could be down as passengers as well," I said. He looked puzzled and produced another list.

"Ahh, here you are," he said, "but what's with all this gear?"

"We won the competition and we asked if we could play on board as well as being passengers," I explained.

"You do know that this is a bridge cruise, don't you?" He said.

"A bridge cruise, what's a bridge cruise?" I queried.

"Exactly what it says. The people who have booked this voyage to the Med are all bridge players, which means they will be playing cards for most of the voyage and by the way, the average age is about sixty-five," he added with a grin.

This left us wondering what people were doing playing bridge on a ship in the ocean, when they could just as easily do it at home. But if you had the money, I suppose you could do whatever you wanted.

We were issued with our cabins Bobby and I shared one and Lee and Charlie the other on "C deck." Jimmy and Alan had decided to join their wives on "E deck" as they could only afford the cheaper berths.

As soon as we could we started exploring the ship. At the top, at the front (bow) of the ship, just under the bridge, was a cocktail lounge called "The Crow's Nest." Bobby and I decided to check it out. As we entered the bar we noticed how posh it looked. There was even a guy dressed in a white suit playing a white piano in the corner. The barman, resplendently dressed in red and gold livery, eyed us up and down with a scathing look.

"Yes sirs," he said in a tone that was not meant to be welcoming, as he continued to clean a glass with a cloth, giving it all his attention.

"Two pints of your best beer please," I said.

"I'm sorry sir, but you are not allowed to be served wearing jeans in this lounge," he told us drily.

We apologised and trooped all the way down to our cabin to change into slacks. Fifteen minutes later we were back.

"Can we have two pints of beer please," I ordered again.

"I'm sorry sir, but jackets are required as dress code in this room," came the reply, with a smirk on his face. All the way back down to the cabin again to find jackets and to save any farther problems, we went the whole hog, donning shirts and ties as well. Feeling we had covered all the angles that the smart bastard could throw at us, we returned once more to the lounge.

"Two pints, please," I requested, with a smug look on my face.

The barman continued to wipe clean his glassware.

"I'm sorry sir, we only serve half pints here."

The "Canberra" had only recently done away with its first and second class segregation, and we were seated with the other cabaret artistes in what was formally the first class dining room.

As we were performing on board, Jimmy and Alan's wives were allowed to join us for meals there. Topping the bill on the ship was Craig Douglas, who had had hits such as "Only Sixteen" in the sixties. He was a really nice guy, and made us "sea rookies" feel welcome.

As a seasoned entertainer on the cruise ships he gave us good advice on the protocol for dinner and the like. Everyone "dressed" for dinner and as we didn't have a great selection of suitable clothes, we would swap our jackets and trousers around to make it look as though we each had a large wardrobe. The meals were unbelievably extravagant, with fifteen courses being the norm.

As the ship pulled out of Southampton

harbour heading for the med, a brass band played on the quayside, and a cascade of paper streamers drifted down, making it a special "Bon voyage" for us sea goers.

"Reminds me of that Titanic film" said Charlie thoughtfully. We settled down to our short life at sea and found that the bar at the sharp end of the ship (the bow,) would close at nine in the morning to restock and be cleaned.

By the time we staggered to the bar at the blunt end (the stern,) it was just opening for business. Although we were never rowdy or making a nuisance of ourselves, we were eyed with extreme suspicion by the sedate bridge playing passengers.

On the second night at sea, we found four kindred spirits in the disco bar. These guys were all young travel agents and had won their free trip on board due to the amount of trips they had sold over the year.

"It's like a floating geriatric ward" said one of the lads. We all agreed that we couldn't be more out of place but were determined to make the most of it.

I wandered over to the bar to get some drinks.

"Six beers, two vodkas and two Lagers please," I ordered.

"That will be two pounds forty-eight, sir." Surely the guy had made a mistake, but I said nothing as I grabbed the laden tray and headed back to our table.

"Excuse me sir" called the barman after me, damn! I knew it was too good to be true, "are you registered as crew?" he asked.

"Yes," I replied.

"Then you are entitled to twenty five percent discount," he told me, handing over the extra change. I got the feeling that this cruise might not be so bad after all.

If there was ever a guy in the wrong job more than the resident DJ on board was, I have yet to find him. He was very public school and when he found out how we had come to be on "his ship," he began to make snide remarks about us publicly over the microphone, commenting how, in certain areas, the standards had dropped drastically on board. This infuriated Bobby the most, causing him to threaten to "slap the twat."

There were some young girls in the crowd that he was trying to impress with this tactic and he was having a limited success with a few of the more snobbish ones. As for the rest, they joined us at our table and were of a similar opinion as ourselves that he was a real prat.

As was the custom on board, the passengers every whim was catered for, and he was obliged to play requests for records when asked.

So began our revenge on our DJ which was to last the entire voyage. We had a copy of the Guinness Book of Hit Singles with us on board and began scouring through the pages to find the most obscure hits we could find. This was because our DJ had cockily announced that he had such a vast collection of records and that he prided himself of never having missed a request in his entire career.

The next night, armed with three unmemorable song titles each, we arrived at the disco. When request time came, Bobby shot out of his chair and dashed to the D.J. booth with a request for an unknown South American band, which had had a small hit in the charts from many years ago. Our disc jockey looked at him blankly and whispered to him that he had never heard of them.

"But you said you had every record ever made in your collection," said Bobby, very loudly for everyone to hear.

"Well, I haven't got that one, so pick another," he hissed. Bobby's next request was for another equally obscure artiste.

"Ha, ha, well it seems that I haven't got that one either," he said, getting quite flustered.

"But that one is my favourite song!" Whined Bobby, "we play it all the time, don't we boys?" he said, looking over at our table.

We all nodded enthusiastically. "Well, we'll just have to wait until you perform it, and maybe then I'll get a copy," he said acidly, "now please sit down and give someone else a chance."

Bobby made a big show of looking dejected as he slowly made his way back to our table.

"Everybody knows that song," he muttered as he passed the other tables.

"Are there any other requests ladies and gentlemen?" our intrepid disc jockey asked, looking relieved at dismissing the thorn in his side that had been Bobby. We had provided one of our female friends with another batch of "unknowns" and she set off to the booth. His smile froze when she asked for yet another obscure song.

"I'm sorry," he apologised, "but I seem to be having difficulty with the requests tonight, so I will have to leave this slot until tomorrow evening."

We sat with huge grins on our faces, enjoying his acute embarrassment and left the disco in triumph. As the nights went by with similar requests, he twigged our little scheme, and ruled that only written requests would accepted by him, which gave him a chance to change the song to his liking, while keeping the complaints from us drowned out by the music.

We retaliated by writing dire threats on the request slips, ranging from throwing him in the pool, or throwing him overboard! (This was the most popular amongst us.) He must have taken our threats seriously because, when we docked in Southampton in the early hours of the morning at the end of the cruise, we were told that he had been almost the first person to leave the ship.

As the days went by we had docked at Palma, Majorca and were just about to arrive at Ajaccio in Corsica. Here we would perform our show in the ship's theatre. A packed house greeted us and we were amazed to receive a tumultuous reception.

Suddenly everyone wanted to know us. The temperature outside was in the high nineties and our stage suits were wet through with sweat when we were finished. Having changed into T-shirts and jeans, we were ushered into the "Crow's Nest" for a drink by the entertainments officer.

"Isn't there a jacket, slacks and tie policy in this lounge?" I asked.

"Normally", he said, "but just this once we'll ignore it." (Ah fame).

For the rest of the cruise, which took in Cannes, Barcelona, and Malaga, we were treated like stars. Everyone greeted us with friendly nods and smiles. Only in the disco area was there a frosty reception and as you may guess, always from the same person. The crew had got to hear about the show and our waiter asked us if we would do a show for them.

Two nights later, we lugged our gear down into the crew's recreation area and did a repeat performance for them. We knew that the vast majority of them were gay but it was still a shock to see most of them in dresses and make-up, sitting in the front row. One crewman in particular had taken a shine to Lee and asked him if he would like a drink.

"I'll have a vodka," said Lee. He returned with a pint glass full to the brim. (Obviously trying to get our lad pissed and have his way with him.)

"There's no orange in it," said Lee. He flicked the glass, allowing the tiniest drop of alcohol to spill from it and replaced it with orange. (God loves a trier!)

While we were having a drink with one of the officers who had come to see the show, he told us an amusing story. A few years previously on the ship, there had been a resident jazz trio. Part of their contract was to stay topside to mix with the passengers and answer questions about their music, etc. There were regular complaints about the bass player, who regarded this as a chore and would escape below decks at the earliest opportunity. Having received his final warning, with the threat of a possible financial penalty to his wages, he grudgingly sat in the music bar after his performance to await the customer's queries.

An American lady of considerable size and wealth approached him.

"Are you one of those music guys?" she

asked.

"Yes Madam," he replied.

"Tell me, what do you do during the day?" she asked.

"Well, I get up about midday, have some lunch, maybe rehearse with the band and then go to the bar for a few."

"No, no," she interrupted, "you must have a proper job, like swabbing the decks, or serving drinks, or something."

"No madam," the bass player said testily, "that's what I'm employed by P and O to do."

"So, you just play in the band as your only job?" came the reply. (To a professional musician, this is a real slap in the face.)

"Yes Madam, now can I ask you what your husband does for a living?" he asked, trying to control himself.

"Well actually, my husband's in oil," she replied importantly.

"What is he, a fucking pilchard!" he snarled. Bass player and suitcase were offloaded at the next port of call.

The cruise came to an end all too soon, and as we loaded our gear into our van and drove out of Southampton docks back to the real world, we took a last look at The Canberra, which had been our home for the last two weeks and left with fond memories which would last a lifetime. It was with great sadness that I read many years later of her last voyage, and subsequent trip to the breakers yard.

Chapter Ten
Black Gold

As the seventies rolled on we consolidated our position as the top cabaret band in Scotland and even ventured over the border into England on a few occasions. These trips were pretty rare because of our full-time jobs.

Never the less, we were working more than a fair percentage of the professional acts. Certain instances stick out in your mind over the years. We were performing in a nightclub in central Scotland. Jimmy was now doing a spoof take off of Elvis. He would appear in a Las Vegas jump suit outfit, complete with the tassels, sequins, and the big belt.

As the music got louder and more frenzied and as he shook his body more wildly, things started to fall off the costume. Little things at first, some sequins, a tassel or two, then the belt would unravel and fall, followed by a sleeve then a trouser leg. The finale being the sideburns curling up the side of his face, which made him look like he had curlers in his hair, before he whipped the Elvis wig off to reveal a bald head.

On this occasion it was met with stony silence. As we stood looking at each other, wondering what could have gone wrong; a man leapt up from the front row and began raining blows on poor Jimmy.

"He's dead you bastard, he's dead," he screamed. While we had been doing our "thing with the king," Elvis had been found dead and the news flashed all over the globe. We were the only people who didn't know.

Jimmy was receiving most of the attention in the band and being the most popular it was only a matter of time before he was lured to a solo career again. The inevitable happened in early nineteen seventy-nine and with a lot of alteration and rehearsals we were able to make the show work as a five-piece unit. After a few weeks ironing out the flaws as we performed, we were back on track with a strong show again.

By this time, three of the guys had given up their day jobs and had become fully professional. Only Alan and I were still working during the day. There was more than enough work to give us a good standard of living, so, after discussing the matter with my wife and being told to "do what you want," I decided to quit my job.

Alan, on the other hand, had a really good job with the Post Office, and after a talk with his missus, had reluctantly decided not to follow the path the rest of the band had taken. Once again Alan and I went our separate ways and we recruited a Musselburgh lad called Freddie, who jumped at the chance to join.

Oil had been found in the North Sea off

Scotland and so began a "Klondike" period, which would last for a few years. With the oil came money and as in the old days of the gold mines, men came to make their fortune, being paid handsome wages.

Many of the work sites were in remote places and efforts were made to keep the workforce entertained, to enable them to endure the harsh environment. The Orkney Isles at the furthermost region beckoned us with the promise of a huge fee and so a week was organised there. There hadn't been much entertainment other than the local talent, previous to our trip and we were told the islanders were looking forward to a visit from a "big act" from Scotland's capital.

The equipment went on ahead with the roadies by road and then by ferry, whilst we would come by air two days later.

We felt like international stars as we boarded the six-seater Cessna light aircraft at Dice airport in Aberdeen for our flight to the island. Our pilot was an American whom I thought had a slight speech impediment, until I sat beside him in the co-pilots seat in the plane. It was then, in the enclosed space of the cockpit, that the strong odour of whisky fumes filled the air. We looked worriedly at each other and then at our pickled pilot, who by this time had started the engine and was taxiing onto the runway.

Either way there was no going back, so

we settled into our seats and pulled our safety belts a notch tighter. Once in the air, our intrepid (smashed) aviator set course for the Orkneys and on reaching open sea, switched on the automatic pilot and promptly fell into a deep, drunken sleep!

This was more than worrying for us, because, if he missed the Orkneys, we roughly reckoned the next piece of terra firma would be Iceland and looking at the half full fuel gauge in front of me, that looked like a very long shot. Apart from the engine, there was no sound to be heard in the cockpit, as we each and everyone, were making mental notes as to what we should have done to be a better person before meeting our maker.

After a while, we started to make as much noise as we could to rouse our airman, but he just slept through it like a newborn baby. A frantic search for life jackets proved futile and still the little Cessna droned on, holding its pre-programmed course. Suddenly, on the horizon, we could see the island in sight. As if an alarm clock had gone off in his head our man awoke with a start, stretched his arms, yawned wearily, switched off the auto-pilot and began his descent. With a much practiced manoeuvre (you could say he could do it in his sleep - nearly!) he landed, applied the brakes and spun the aircraft around, barely twenty feet from the end of the runway and the open sea. After taxiing to his parking spot, he switched the engine off, jumped out, wished us well and hoped we enjoyed the flight, then staggered off to the airport bar to top up on his alcohol intake.

A frantic phone call was made to Mike to re-arrange our return journey. A unanimous decision was made to return by the ferry boat.

Four concerts had been arranged on the islands, with the final one to be staged in the main town of Kirkwall. The first three had gone down really well and we were looking forward to the final performance. As we pulled up to the front of the hall, we were met by a very small man with a very big clipboard.

"Hello there, I'm Andrew," he said. "I'll be in charge of your electrics," he said importantly.

"That's ok, we have our own crew for that," said Freddie.

"No, I'm in charge of the building electrics," he informed us. Assuming that he was the house electrician, we left it at that.

Once the equipment was set up and we were ready for a sound check, little Andrew appeared with his big clipboard again. He approached me and asked, "how many watts power is your amplifier?"

"Two hundred watts," I informed him. He looked skywards in deep concentration, tapping his pencil on his cheek. "Hmmm, that could be as much as half a bag," he calculated, scribbling away on his board.

The rest of the equipment received the same conversion from watts to bags and with his information copied on to his giant clipboard, Andrew went home for his tea, leaving us none the wiser about his activities.

The time for the concert approached and Andrew re-appeared, dressed in a black tuxedo and bow tie. You would think he was having a night at the opera. The only thing missing was the white silk scarf. With him he had brought a foldaway stool and five very large canvas bags. As we took our positions just before the curtain was opening, Andrew followed us on and with a theatrical sweep of his hands, unfolded the stool at the rear of the stage. Armed with his bags, which were full of five pence pieces, he positioned himself on the stool by the slot which fed the coin-operated electric meter and began to insert coins one by one. As the show progressed, and the meter indicator whizzing around at a manic speed, Andrew never flinched and stuck manfully to his task.

At the end of the show, after our encore (and five empty coin bags later,) Andrew was called forward for his own personal bow, which he majestically took, cheered on by his adoring public.

"The bastard got a better reception than us," said Freddie ruefully.

The next trip took us to Sullom Voe in the

Shetlands. There were two camps there for the workers. We, being cabaret, were given accommodation on the M.V. Rangaterra, a ship moored in the bay next to the camps. It was used to house the managers and foremen of the work sites. The cabins were very plush and spacious, so much better than the portacabins on the shore.

We regarded ourselves very lucky until one of the crew told us that the ship had once been used as a ferry between the two main islands of New Zealand until her sister ship had gone down, with a heavy loss of life. It was found that a fault in design on the rear cargo doors had caused the ship to sink and therefore the Rangaterra had been de-commissioned immediately afterwards. From then on I didn't sleep so soundly in my comfy cabin, as any sound of running water had me reaching for a life jacket.

Sullom Voe was a desolate place with little or nothing to break the monotony, so the men worked and drank hard. There always seemed to be a wind blowing and when it rained (which was most of the time we were there) the rain came sideways. You would see men walking crab style, with their backs soaking wet, while their fronts were perfectly dry.

There were only four trees in the whole area, pathetic little scrubby things, little more than bushes. They were situated in a local man's garden and he protected them fiercely to the extent of building an electric fence around them to ward off any thieves. As I said, the men worked hard, and drank hard, so hard it appeared that they had only been in the area for a few days before they had been barred from the only bar there.

Faced with the thought of no pub for many, many miles, they came up with a solution. They would build their own pub. Building materials were in plentiful supply, and it was agreed that the men would build it on the days they were not working. On paper this looked like a sound plan as there would be at least fifty men available on any given day.

A time prediction was given at one week at the most from the onset of the build. Unfortunately, the days that the men had off was also their big drinking day and they would arrive on site with their tools, and at least ten cans of beer each.

As the day wore on, technical problems such as straight walls and corners meeting were glossed over. After two and a half weeks of this drunken chaos, there it stood. Every wall had a significant lean, and the roof slanted at a jaunty angle, but it was mainly dry inside, and it was theirs. Nobody cared that it broke every building regulation in the book as they drank their beer and spirits from the bar counter with a twenty-degree slope.

During the visit there we had to change the act accordingly to suit the needs of these oil workers. It went from a slick nightclub act to downright x-rated porn movie material. The customer is always right as they say and if you want to work (and keep these particular crazy guys happy,) you give 'em what they want.

Armed with this "mature" show, our next forage north was to a little village called Kishorn, high up on the west coast. They had built a camp a few miles outside and had dug a massive purpose built hole in one of the inlets there, to be able to build oil rigs, and float them directly out to sea. As we approached the picturesque little village we saw a taste of what we were in for.

The village itself consisted of a few crofter style cottages and a small general store, cum post office. Directly by the dirt track road leading to the camp was a brand-new police station, which was almost as big as the rest of the village combined. (We found out later, there were eighteen holding cells inside).

As we drove up the track we passed a trail of wrecked cars on either side. Most of them were brand new! Later, when the weather got bad and the track started to subside, they gathered up all the wrecks and crushed them down to lay a solid foundation for the road. Turning into the camp, we were met with a sight of intense activity, which seemed alien to the peaceful silence of the surrounding area.

There were giant overhead cranes swinging to and fro, fetching materials, and men in hardhats banging and drilling everywhere. All were scurrying around like human ants around the skeleton framework of a massive oil rig rising up out in the manmade bay.

Our host was there to greet us. He was a mountain of a man, at least six feet six tall, with an uncanny resemblance to Bluto, the baddie in the Popeye cartoons.

"Welcome to Kishorn lads," he said. "Home to the "commando's. That's the name these bunch of unwashed, unruly, jailbait bastards call themselves". "I hope you've had experience of this type of audience before or they will rip you up for arse paper."

I told him we had done the Orkneys and the Shetlands and had no problem.

"That's as well may be lad, but up here all these wankers have got is good food and plenty of drink."

He had been there from the start and told us that, at the beginning there were a few local lasses around to "entertain" them. As the camp grew and more and more men arrived, this led to fights among them to win the female favours.

"They would shag your granny's grannies if they got the chance, that's why we had to put a ban on any women near the camp," he said. "The only solution we can find at the moment is to fill their bellies with the best of grub and give them two hours after their shift to drink themselves stupid, that way it keeps the fights down to about four a night."

"They make good money then?" I asked.

"It's coming out of their ears", he replied.

"What's with all the smashed cars we saw on the road up?" Lee asked.

"They buy new cars, get pissed, crash them, and rather than arse about getting them fixed, they go out and buy another one," said Bluto. "To give you an idea of how much money they make, even the lad who washes the dishes is on six hundred a week!" (Remember, this was in the early eighties.)

He took us to the Portacabins where we would be staying and then took us to the hall we would be playing. As we entered, we saw a bar worker sweeping broken glass off the stage. By the looks of it, there was more than one glass that had been shattered.

"That was from last night," he smirked, "didn't like the singer, thought he was shit."

As we passed by the stage, the barman beckoned to Bluto, "I hope this lots alright, we're running out of glasses." Bluto turned to us, ignoring the barman.

"You'll be doing two shows a day, one for the day shift at nine o' clock at night, and one for the night shift at nine o' clock in the morning."

"Nine in the morning? We'll never get up

at that time!" said Lee.

"Oh yes you will because I'll be dragging you out of your scratchers at eight thirty," growled our host.

We were booked for two days as we wouldn't be able to entertain all the people on the two shifts in one go. As we prepared for the first night show, we went to the bar for some Dutch courage.

"Can't serve till quarter to nine," our barman said sharply, "that's when the door opens."

We looked at the clock. Twenty-five to nine. The main entrance had a double-door with a two-inch thick metal bar looped through the security notches. On closer inspection I noticed the bar had a distinct bend, due to heavy pressure applied from the other side of the door over a period of time.

Through the end of the bar was tied a stout rope, which ran all the way back to the bar counter. As the clock neared the quarter hour, the staff began furiously pouring pints and spirits, and stacking them on the bar top.

"Right, let the bastards in," ordered Bluto. With that, one of the staff yanked the rope, pulling the metal bar free.

The door burst open and a horde of unshaven filthy workers in their muddy overalls and boots and still wearing their hard hats, spilled into the room.

They made a beeline for the bar, throwing money over and scooping up as many drinks as they could carry back to the wooden tables in the hall. Within two minutes the room was packed, and the noise was deafening. There were people there from all over the U.K. and farther afield, such as Norway, Holland, and the like.

"You're on in five minutes," yelled Bluto over the noise, "good luck."

There was no dressing room to change in so we were standing there in our stage clothes ready to go. This drew a lot of attention from the filthy rabble, who began to heckle us, and shout dire threats our way. By the time we were ready to go on we had the overwhelming feeling of Christians being thrown to the lions.

We need not have worried. As we were only doing a one-hour set, we condensed the show and put in all the powerful musical impressions, leaving out anything that would give the crowd a chance to bait us. We came off to thunderous applause, with beer mugs being crashed down in a crescendo of noise on the wooden tables, and roars and whistles echoing through the hall. Still in our stage gear, we were grabbed and pushed to the bar by our newly found adoring crowd. Pints of beer and all manner of spirits came at us from all angles, with the order to "get 'em down our necks!"

With the relief of having put on a good show, and the pressure taken off us we duly obliged.

After a few pints a little guy pushed his way through the crowd and banged a metal bucket on the bar by us.

"Here," he said. "This is for you."

We looked inside the bucket; it was full of coins, five pound and ten-pound notes.

"What's this for?" I asked.

"We had a whip-round," he answered.

"But we are getting paid for the show already!" I said.

"Yeah, but they are paying you shit-pence, so we thought we would make your wages up a bit," he answered. (We were being paid twelve hundred pounds, plus expenses for the two days, and we thought that it was a very good deal.)

As the bar was only open for another half hour after the show, we could see why the workers were drinking as much and as fast as they could. Closing time came and Bluto could be heard yelling, "do your talking while you're walking," to the drunken rabble.

With only two miner scuffles and a fist fight over the whole period, he was well satisfied with the quiet night.

"We used to stay open until two in the morning," he informed us, "but the stupid bastards were so pissed, they were falling off the scaffolding the next day, we were losing two a week, so we cut the drinking time down," he added.

As the main bar was closed and the bar staff began clearing away the mountain of empty glasses and cans, he ushered us into the next room.

"This is the lounge" he said. It looked just as basic as the main hall we had just left. "It used to have carpets and drapes, but after a couple of nights they were soaked through with blood and snot and we had to throw the lot of it out," our host said. "I tell you, I've picked up teeth, bits of skin and even an eye once", he added, "but anyway, what would you like to drink lads?" As he took his place behind the bar.

We had taken the bucket full of cash through to the lounge with us and on Bluto's insistence, began counting the money. Three hundred and eighty pounds!

We were all taken aback by the amount. "Aye, they definitely like you," said Bluto "and now that word has got round the camp, I've no doubt you'll get the same at the morning show!"

This was, by a long way, an unexpected bonus for us (and no commission to come out of it either.) As we sat and drank with the big man, he told us one of the stories about the camp. One story in particular involved an overhead crane driver. He had worked off the coast of Norway prior to coming to Kishorn and had been involved in a fatal accident there. Apparently, as he was lifting a load, the chains holding it had snapped, dropping the load and killing some workers directly below. By the time he arrived at the camp a rumour had gone around the compound, saying he had held a grudge, and dropped the load on purpose.

The "killer" crane man was very upset to hear these unfounded rumours about him and tried in vain to explain what really happened. Having tried for a week or so with no success he decided to capitalise on his notoriety. He passed the word around the workforce below him that it would cost each of them five pounds a day to ensure a similar fate didn't befall them.

As there were an average of three hundred men toiling below every day, this turned into a very lucrative project, so much so, that he bought five houses in his home town with the proceeds!

After a long while, our host told us that it was three in the morning and we had better get some shut- eye to be fresh for the nine- o- clock morning show. We staggered back in a drunken state to our portacabin and still in our stage suits, collapsed on our bunks, and slept the sleep of the comatose.

We were rudely awakened by Bluto banging on the metal walls of the cabin, shouting "come on lads, the night shift are waiting for you!"

My head felt as though it was encased in lead and my eyes had broken glass behind them.

We lurched to our feet and headed for the hall in our crumpled stage suits. (Well at least that save some time!)

"Bloody hell!" Thundered Bluto, (as fresh as a daisy, the bastard!) "you look fucking awful the lot of you, here drink this, it'll get you through the show." He thrust a coffee mug into each of our shaking hands. We gulped down the hot brew and I suddenly felt as though someone had started a fire in my belly. We all began retching and coughing.

"What the fuck was in that?" I screamed. "Navy rum" came the answer, "kill or cure you," he added. It certainly seemed to cure us as the potent brew quickly took effect.

The morning show went as well as the previous evening's and the bucket was duly passed around again. This time there was over four hundred pounds in it. After the obligatory drinks with Bluto again, we were ushered in to the dining hall. The food smelt delicious and we realised that we hadn't eaten since early the day previously.

As I moved up the queue (in my even more grubby stage suit) three enormous T- bone steaks were slammed onto my plate, followed by a mountain of mashed potato, Brussels sprouts, roast spuds, and a lake of gravy.

Ravenous though I was and buckling under the weight of the food I was carrying, I asked what I was to do with it all.

"Fucking eat it!" Came the bored reply.

The rest of the day was spent sleeping off the huge quantities of food and drink we had consumed. I woke up later in the afternoon and decided to go for a snack in the meal hall. (Never turn down the chance to eat when you're a travelling band, as you never know when you'll get fed again.)

I opened the cabin door and stepped out into a thick mist. You couldn't see your hand in front of your face, it was that thick. As I walked down the cabin steps the mist disappeared and I realised that it was hanging just a few inches above my head. It was the weirdest natural phenomenon I had ever seen. When I reached the hall I was greeted like an old friend. Apparently we were one of them now, due to our no- nonsense (and bloody filthy) show.

An incident had occurred that afternoon which had the whole camp talking about it. It seemed that one of the American overseers had demanded, (not asked) to inspect a part of the rig being built out in the bay. This involved him being hoisted by crane in a metal cage and swung high over the waters to the rig.

He was new to the camp, but already had upset many of the workforce with his superior attitude towards them. The crane driver he had spoken to in an off-handed manner had seemingly bowed to his demands without a whimper.

Having handed the man a Walkie-Talkie to keep in touch with his orders he jumped into the cage and barked "lift!" The driver duly raised the cage high into the air. "Left!" ordered the yank. The crane began slowly swinging out to the right, away from the rig and out into the centre of the bay.

"Left goddamit, not right!" Yelled the American. The crane continued its slow journey right. "Don't you know your left from your right, you stupid limey bastard!" Screamed the overseer. The cage came to a halt, swinging gently over the middle of the bay and then ever so slowly began descending.

"What the fuck are you doing?" Yelled the Yank into the Walkie-Talkie. The cage continued its downward path with the man screaming orders in vain, until it sank beneath the surface. After about thirty seconds it re-appeared from the freezing waters with a very wet and cold overseer clinging to the sides of the cage in terror. The cage was then carefully brought back to the shore and gently laid onto the ground beside a group of workers, collapsed in a heap of laughter. The furious sodden man struggled out of the cage and threatened the driver with immediate dismissal. (This action was dropped when he was informed he might have a great load descend from the skies on to his head as the driver had done it before!)

The second evening show came to an end

with more money in the bucket, but this time we held back on the drink as we were leaving straight after the following morning's show. Bluto said his farewells that evening as he would be gone by seven the next morning to pick up supplies for the camp.

"You'll have no problem now lads, the men have really taken to you," our host said as he shook us by the hand and bade us a fond farewell.

The following morning, with the show over (and another bucket of cash to count) we loaded up our gear and headed out of camp. As we passed the guys grafting away on the rig the men waved and whistled to us as we passed, wishing us all the best. On the long journey home we tallied up the money from the buckets we had been given. There was over sixteen hundred pounds in the kitty! This was more than the original fee we had charged for the shows, which made it a very profitable few days indeed.

We would visit the camp again later in the year, and this time there was a caravan site set up just outside the gates. The caravans were occupied by a gang of prostitutes, cashing in on the big money being made by the men. The guys called the cluster of caravans "the happy land." With these "comforts" close to hand, the fights had diminished noticeably, and the authorities, happy to see a marked improvement in the law and order in the area, had turned a blind eye to the extra facilities.

I will always have fond memories of these men. They were a hard-working, hard-drinking, hard-living breed. Sadly, most had come with the dream of making lots of money and plans of a life of luxury after only a few years. Unfortunately, the hard life forced many to turn to drink and gambling to make things bearable and the vast majority never realised their dreams.

Chapter Eleven
Nookie Brown and Stottie Cakes

We returned home to find we had been booked for a ten-day run in the North East of England. A ten-day run incorporated two weekends and the week between. In this way the agent would make good money for you at the weekends and that would cover the weekdays when the money was not as good.

The North East was regarded as the birthplace of club land, and as a comedy act, this was going to be a tough initiation. It was a well known fact that if you could succeed with comedy in Newcastle, Middlesbrough, and surrounding areas, you could take your act anywhere. This was our first real venture into England and we were up for the challenge ahead.

We had been given digs in a farmhouse near Spennymoor, County Durham, by the local agent who had booked us. They were known in the business as "pro digs." This meant that all the residents were cabaret acts doing their rounds of the clubs in the area. As this was all new to us recent professionals, it was quite a shock to find that the six of us had to share one room. Breakfast was from eleven in the morning, and tea was served at five in the evening. The landlady had devised this timetable to accommodate the fact that the acts wouldn't get back from their gigs until at least one in the morning and would have to be on the road for the gigs by six at the latest. The digs were clean, basic, and cheap, which was all that was required by anyone in the business.

Having arrived in time to settle in and sit in for tea, we asked the other experienced acts about the kind of audience we could expect.

"They're all bastards!" One fellow told me. "They don't like anything and if by chance they do, then they won't even show it. Your best bet is to get your head down, do your show, pick up the money and get to fuck out as soon as possible."

"But we do a lot of comedy in our act, so surely that should win them over?" I said.

The whole table burst into whoops of laughter.

"Comedy! You poor bastards! That's the worst," giggled our learned thespian. "Where's your first gig?" he asked.

"The red house in Middlesbrough" we told him.

"Oh my god" he looked at us with sympathy in his eyes, "they've really dropped you guys in the shit with that one."

Everyone around the table murmured in agreement. "That cesspit must be one of the worst in the North East, we won't do it any more will we?" He asked the rest of the acts, who all nodded back at him. "Anyway, good luck, you'll need it, and don't forget, if you get paid off before the end of the night, you still get the full fee, so don't let them short change you".

Armed with these cheery words of encouragement we set off for Middlesbrough. The club looked pretty run-down from the outside and not much better inside. The stage had a six-inch high wire fence at the front of it for some reason. As we set up, the concert secretary came to greet us.

"I thought you were a three-piece," he said. We assured him we were a five-piece unit. He looked puzzled.

"I don't remember you being jocks," he said in his heavy "Geordie" accent.

"Well, considering we come from Scotland, I think we are," Lee sarcastically replied.

"Wait just a minute, you're not the Ivy League are you?" our host inquired.

"No, we are the Mimics," I said.

"Fucking hell, this lot are expecting the Ivy League!" he said with panic in his voice, motioning toward the crowd starting to fill the hall.

"They've paid fifty pence cover charge for tonight, they'll go bloody mad if it's not the Ivy League!"

The Ivy League had had a few hits in the sixties and had made the transition to comedy band with great success. They had built up a large following in clubland throughout Britain and were popular wherever they went.

It became apparent that the local agent we were working for had found them a better paid venue and had swapped us for them at the last moment.

"Let's not panic," said our troubled friend, (panicking) "I'll just have to explain to them out there what's happened, so before you go on, I'll go out front, tell them the score, and give you a big build up."

We thanked him for his help and promised to give him a good account of ourselves.

Showtime! And as we waited nervously behind the stage curtain, our host stuck his head through the drapes from the front of the stage.

"All right lads?" he asked. "I am just gonna make the announcement then you're on, okay?"

We nodded and waited for his big build up. "Ladies and gentlemen, can I have your attention please?" Requested the man, silencing the crowd.

"As you know, tonight we were supposed to have the Ivy League, a brilliant comedy band, who we've had here many times and I'm sure you'll agree the best comedy act that's ever set foot in this club". He took a deep breath.

"Unfortunately, the bastards have cancelled, so we've got this Scotch crap instead.

take it away lads!" With that, the curtains flew open, revealing five stunned Scots caught unawares by the swiftness of his actions. We went into our act with our tried and tested comedy routines. Nothing, only stoney silence. We went into our music breaks. Nothing. We came off the stage after our first spot to the sound of our own feet. We sat in the dressing room in total despair, wanting the ground to swallow us up. If we had been offered the chance to make a break for it, leaving everything behind, I think at that moment, we would have jumped at it.

The dressing room door opened and our committee man entered.

"All right bonny lads?" He asked with a grin, "you'll be back on in about fifty minutes for your dance spot." I looked at him in disbelief.

"You want us back on?" I asked.

"Why aye man, certainly," he answered. "But they hated us, we died on our arses out there," I said.

"Naw man, it's just that they've seen it all and heard it all, so they don't get too excited (understatement) and anyway, they must like yer, they're staying for the bingo!" This was our first introduction to the North East and over the coming years we came to adapt ourselves to the local humour.

As we walked into the digs that night we were met by the other acts, anxious to find out how the "new boys" had got on, on their first night. We told them what had happened and they seemed suitably impressed.

"Tony over there only lasted five minutes with those bastards," one of the acts told us, "and I only lasted about twenty myself," he added.

We are a strange breed we cabaret acts. We call each other behind our backs, tell whopping great lies about how good we are, but we generally stick together as a unit against "them" (Them being the general public.)

The clubs at that time were at their peak in popularity in the North East and we worked every night on our ten-day run, with the final show being a Sunday afternoon slot. (It was said there was one street with at least ten clubs on it, and you could do your whole ten days on it.)

As we packed our gear and headed back up the road on our three-hour journey home we felt well satisfied with the gigs we had done, and looked forward to returning, but we also looked forward to some privacy and sleeping in our own beds. Having said that, I was virtually a lodger in my own home and generally came and went with little or no communication with my wife.

It was time for a trip to the North of Scotland again with the venues being Inverness, Elgin, and Fort William. It is said that the best spoken English in the whole of the United

Kingdom is spoken in Inverness. The women sounded virginal with their soft-spoken accent, but were anything but, as we found out on our first night there. As gigs go, we had gone down exceptionally well and were swamped with eager young girls in the dressing room asking for autographs.

Lee called us to him. "Listen," he said, "why don't we have a little bet?"

"What are you thinking of?" I asked.

"Well, just look at all these women, they are gagging for it, so I reckon the guy who has the most unusual fuck wins and we put a tenner each in the kitty," he explained.

We tossed our tenners in to the pot and went off with our respective dates we had picked up, leaving one of the roadies holding the money. A few hours later when we drifted back to our digs we began to relate our exploits to find who would be the winner. Freddie had had his way on the roof of a factory, while I had done the business in the cramped interior of an M.G. sports car. (No mean feat if I may say.) Charlie had succeeded to gain entry into an empty double decker bus and had put the wide seats at the rear to good use, whilst using his dates foot to press the stop button at every stroke. This gave him extra points in everyone's opinion. Lee had somehow found a lake with a canoe on it, and rocked the boat, so to speak.

Up to that point it was agreed that it was

a close call between Charlie and Lee, when suddenly Bobby burst through the door. The knees of his trousers were ripped to shreds, as were the elbows of his shirt. Blood was dripping from all four of his joints.

"Where the hell have you been?" I asked.

"Bramble bush," he gasped.

"You are bleeding like a stuck pig," I continued.

"You think that's bad, you ought to see her arse!" He answered.

The roadie holding the money walked over to Bobby, and without a word, thrust the notes into his bloodstained hand.

As soon as we returned home we had another ten day run in the North East lined up for us. This time we were prepared for the reception (or lack of it) from the local crowds. It was comforting to know where we were staying and the farmhouse was fast becoming a second home to us. As we pulled up outside, we noticed three other band vans parked up. We soon got to know the other guys and became friends with them over the next few days.

One band had the area sussed out to perfection. Knowing that if they were "paid off" and still getting their full fee, they had devised a cunning scheme, where they would arrange to have two gigs on the same night. On the first gig they would put on such a shockingly bad show, they were fired almost immediately. A quick dash to the second venue, where a second set of equipment was set up ready to go and they would do their proper act. This of course gave them double the money for the night.

They pulled this scam all around the North East for quite a few years, changing the name of the band every so often so they could play the same clubs again and again.

"Has it ever backfired on you?" I asked one of the band.

"Only once," he replied. "We were at a club in Chester-Le-Street and we kicked off, all out of tune playing the wrong chords, you know the score, anyway, we had got through the first number and none of the committee had come near us, so we broke into our second number, which was worse than the first. Still nobody came to drag us off the stage. We played our whole first set and by that time, even we couldn't fucking stand it! At the break I asked one of the committee if it was ok."

"Why man that was absolute shite!" he answered"

"Then why didn't you pay us off?"

He said, "Well, we were waiting to see if you got any better!"

Before we left for the gig that night, the landlady asked us to do her a favour. A female duo had turned up unexpectedly and were desperate for somewhere to stay. Would we mind if she put them with us, in our room?

Would we mind? Oh no, not in the slightest.

After the gig it was normal to take a few beers back and sit in the large lounge, filled with settees and talk about things that had happened to everyone on their travels. The other bands and acts were already there and as we chatted, we kept looking to the door to see the girls arrive. At last they made an appearance. Two of the most gorgeous blond beauties you could ever see, with figures to die for.

After talking for a while, it was time for bed. We did the gentlemanly thing and let our "roomies" go up to the room first. After a few minutes we followed, leaving our chums on the settees staring at us with envious eyes. As we entered the room, we noticed the double bed in the corner containing our two beauties. We switched off the light, said our good nights and waited to see what would happen next.

We didn't have long to wait as there came sighs and groans of passion from the double bed. Just our fucking luck! Our two darlings were fully paid up members of the lesbian club. This moaning and groaning went on every night for the next four days and was beginning to grate on our nerves. Eventually, on the fourth night we had had enough, and just as our duo reached their climaxes, we all sat up in bed, switched the light on, and gave our sex athletes a rousing round of applause. It didn't stop their future steamy advances toward each other, but at least they were a damn sight quieter!

As we came to the end of the run we were adjusting more and more to the North East humour and were finally getting some laughs here and there.

Our final gig was a night gig at Ferryhill Social club, a big club with a reputation of having a harder than normal audience. We did well and ran a little over time due to two encores. We packed the gear and piled it up by the fire exit door, ready for loading into the van. We gave the dressing room one last check and returned to load up. The fire exit, which had been open, was now firmly shut and bolted, with chains and padlocks wrapped around the handles for good measure.

The less than happy caretaker was waiting for us, arms folded in a business-like manner.

"Come on lads, I'm not paid past eleven-o-clock, let's have yer out!"

"But we've got the gear still to pack," said Bobby.

"Well, ye can do that tomorrow, me suppers on the table!" He said.

"We're driving back to Scotland tonight" said Bobby.

"Not my problem" Insisted our jobs worth, "come back tomorrow dinner time."

"I think you had better open that fire door right now for your own sake!" Bobby said.

"Oh aye, and how's that then?" Came the angry reply.

"Cos if you don't, there are five Scotsmen gonna take these keys off you and ram them up your fucking arse!" yelled Bobby.

A look around at the hostile stares convinced him that we meant business and he hurriedly unlocked the door. Afterwards, we thanked him cordially as he stormed off, muttering something about Scotch bastards keeping him from his supper.

The relationship between our manager Mike and ourselves had been getting more and more strained at that point, due to the fact that he had been taking on more acts on his books, and was even managing two of them. He insisted he could manage to keep all three acts covered, but our argument was that he should concentrate on us as we were his main show.

With other agencies now very interested in us, things came to a head and we decided to part company with him.

We signed up with a bigger agency based in Central Scotland and Adam, our new boss, had contracts throughout the United Kingdom.

He also suggested we do "extras" work for films and TV. The only stumbling block was that we would require Equity union cards to do this work. This was no easy task as it was a "catch twenty-two" situation where, to get your card you had to be working in TV, films, or theatre, but you couldn't work these areas if you didn't have one.

Somehow, Adam managed to get us all provisional Equity cards and within a week we had our first job.

Chapter Twelve
Deutschland Uber Allies

Extras work is by no stretch of the imagination glamorous. It usually meant you made up the crowd in the background to the main actors. You were paid, on average, twenty-five pounds per day, which was good money in the early eighties. You could also add to that income by doing a "speaking" part, which involved you saying a few words, or a "walk-on" part, which meant what it said, by walking on, or through the shot.

Most of the time though, was spent hanging around waiting for the crew to set up the scene, get the light right, and so on.

Our first time was on a show called "Garnock Way" which was the Scottish equivalent of "Coronation Street "in its day. We were cast as a bunch of bricklayers who had gone on strike for better pay and conditions. We were holding a strike meeting in the local pub. The script was for our union shop steward to be standing on a chair, shouting things like, "we want a fair day's pay for a fair day's work" and "we won't be held to ransom by the company!" with us gathered around him, voicing our agreement.

Two of the main actors would then enter the pub, loudly disagreeing with us and stirring up a tense situation between us. The climax was a full-scale brawl between the bricklayers and most of the pub regulars.

After five "takes" the producer was still not happy with the fight scene.

"Look," he said. "You're supposed to be hard, rufty-tufty workmen who have been drinking all afternoon and in no mood for anybody to argue with them. You are just not putting enough rawness into the fight scene."

"How can we act drunk when we haven't had a drink apart from this cordial which is supposed to be beer?" complained one of the extras.

"Right!" Our producer said. "Everybody next door now!" He ordered. We all trooped into the real pub which adjoined the studio. The producer marched up to the bar and said "pour this lot beer or spirits until I tell you to stop, and charge it to the studio." An hour and a half later, with all the cast taking full advantage of the free booze, he felt we were ready.

Back in the studio, we did the scene in one take. The producer got his realistic fight scene, we got happily drunk with pay and apart from one extra who had his jaw broken, another with two teeth missing and a part of the fake bar being destroyed, everybody was happy.

It was a weird feeling, sitting watching myself on the television when it was shown a few days later. My mother (god bless her) was quite distressed when she saw me. "What happened to the band?" She said in a hurt tone. "I thought you were doing really well, why did you pack it in to become a bricklayer?" she said.

It was no use trying to explain to her that it was only an act. She really believed there was a "Garnock Way."

Adam phoned me up a few nights later.

"Have you got a valid passport?"

"Yeh, why?" I said.

"You've got a fortnight in Germany. You'll be working for the armed forces doing Naafi shows."

We had a mad scramble around to get the necessary paperwork for transport in the next day or so, but we managed to obtain all the documents we would need for the journey.

By this time we were using a "box type" transit van to ferry our gear around and although it had seen better days, it was a reliable motor and we had no worries about taking it to Germany. There was an agency that specialised in entertainment for the troops and because they were based in the south of England they used the local port of Felixstowe as their ferry point to the continent.

With us being based in Scotland, this added an extra day to our journey, but as it was a new experience for us, we didn't mind at the time. We took the overnight ferry to Zeebrugge, and after a sleepless night trying to nod off on the chairs next to the fruit machines, we landed in the early hours. (No luxury sleeping cabins for us this time!)

After passing through immigration control, we set off through Belgium, Holland and finally entered Germany. At that time each country had its borders with passport control and this added more time on to our journey. We finally arrived in Aachen on the German border which was to be our first gig of the tour at about six in the evening.

There were no signs to tell us where the army camp was and none of us could speak any German.

"I've learnt some of the lingo" said Lee, flicking through a small German translation book.

"Pull over there beside that guy and I'll ask him" he said.

"Enshuldigung mein Herr, woe its der Britisher soldaten camp bitte?"

We all looked at Lee with admiration, especially when the man answered back in a flood of German.

"Danke, danke," said Lee as we drove off.

"Well? what did he say?" I asked.

"Fucked if I know, I didn't think about him answering me back!" Cried Lee.

Luckily we found a soldier on his way back to camp and he showed us the way.

Naafi shows are normally held in the canteen where the troops eat and drink, so there are never such luxuries as a stage or lighting provided. Fortunately, we had our own lighting with us, but for power, we usually had to unplug one of the many hot food vending machines lined along the walls. This would cause us problems on numerous occasions when drunken "squaddies" would lurch past the band in full swing, pull out our plug, plug in their favourite machine, and bring the show to a sudden halt.

On that first tour, we had a husband and wife musical duo as support. We clicked right away and became firm friends for many years after. It was the first time playing for the armed forces for the both of us, so we didn't know quite what to expect. We didn't have long to wait to find out when they entered the room. They were shouting and screaming abuse at us, even before the show started. The "lions and Christians" feeling came over us, as it had done when we had played for the oil workers.

We decided that a "very mature" show was called for under the circumstances.

The duo went on first and were very good indeed, but you could hardly hear them for the torrent of abuse coming from the crowd. Eventually, Janet, the keyboard player, picked out a particularly noisy lad at the front, and said "I'll tell you what arsehole, if your cock is as big as your mouth, I'll see you in the dressing room later!"

This was greeted with a tremendous cheer and the guy sheepishly slunk back in his seat. From then on, their act went down a storm. This was to be the format for the show and all other shows in the future, and when it was our turn, we followed suit with the filthiest jokes and sketches we could think up. Give 'em what they want, and that's exactly what we did. We ended a very successful evening getting very drunk at the bar with an adoring audience.

We moved on to Dusseldorf, Minden, Bielefeld, Osnabruck, all "garrison" towns as they were called, with our trusty old Transit van doing a sterling job as it lumbered up and down the autobahns.

An incident occurred on our fourth day into the tour involving the German police. As we were travelling along, flat out, at our maximum speed of fifty miles per hour, a green and white police car came up behind us. Suddenly its siren began to wail and its lights began flashing as it overtook us. It pulled sharply up in front of us, bringing us to an abrupt halt, and testing the van's brakes at the same time. One of the policemen got out of the car and approached us, while the other unclipped his holster, drew his pistol and leaning over the car roof, pointed his gun at us sitting in the front of the van.

At this time in Germany, there was a terror group called the Bader Meinhof, who were blowing up buildings, kidnapping, and causing mayhem across the country. This made the police force very edgy and therefore, things like enclosed vans travelling slowly along an autobahn which was designed for speed caused them to be more than a little suspicious.

The officer who was approaching us realised we were from the U.K. And went to the right-hand side of the van. He motioned me to open the sliding door. (Yes, I'm driving again!) Unfortunately, the week before, the door had broken from its hinges and we had welded it shut. I tried to tell him in sign language that it wouldn't open, but this was misunderstood by the cop, who thought that I wasn't going to open it. He angrily banged on the door and motioned again for me to open the door.

"What's German for welded" I pleaded. Charlie was frantically flicking through the German phrase book.

"It's not in here" he informed me. By this time a very irate cop was banging and yelling, and quickly running out of patience. His partner had adjusted his firing position and cocked his pistol, ready for action. I was still trying to show him the problem when he stormed around to the other side of the van, slammed the passenger door back, reached over, and dragged me out of the van by my collar. I was pushed hard against the side of the van and my legs kicked apart.

Charlie and Lee frantically motioned him to look inside at the welded door to show him the problem. His attitude changed instantly, and he rested an arm on my shoulder ad ushered me to the rear of the van.

"Broken!" He said, in bad English, pointing to the offside indicator plastic cover. Peered at the offending unit and could just make out a slight crack in the lens.

"It's only cracked!" I said.

"Broken" he insisted loudly. I decided that it would be no use to argue, as it was clear he was not going to change his point of view. Having admitted the offence, the cop produced a book from his pocket and showed me a diagram of my crime, written in six different languages, explaining why he was going to fine me on the spot.

After parting with thirty Deutschmarks, I was given a receipt for my payment. Before he returned to his partner by the police car, he paused, and said in his thick German accent "if this was a German vehicle, it would not be allowed on our roads."

"We're having a fucking hard time keeping it on the British ones!" Replied Bobby. The cop looked puzzled at first with this answer, then, shaking his head in despair, got into the car with his partner and drove off.

The following day we stopped off in a little village for some lunch. It consisted of one Main Street, stretching left and right as far as the eye could see in a straight line with houses on either side. The rest of the guys were already sitting in the café across the road by the time I had parked the van. I noticed a pedestrian crossing with about fifteen locals waiting for the "green man" to cross over and joined the queue.

After a minute, with no cars coming either way, or none of the Germans making a move, I looked both ways and started walking across. No sooner had I stepped off the kerb, when an ear-piercing whistle rent the air. A policeman had appeared from nowhere and was pulling the dreaded book from his pocket, motioning me to come to him. The locals looked at me with scorn in their eyes as though I had committed a bloodthirsty murder. I looked at the diagram shown to me (in six different languages.) Jaywalking!

Another twenty Deutschmarks changed hands, and another receipt was handed over. As the cop took his leave, he asked "is this your first time in Germany?"

I nodded. He smiled sweetly, "I hope you enjoy your stay here," he added.

"I don't think I can afford it mate, I've only been here a few days and I'm fifty marks down already!"

No sooner had we returned from Germany than we were off to the North East again, and back to the farm. A band from London was staying there for their ten-day run and we became friends with them. We, being

Scottish, regarded ourselves as pretty good drinkers, but these guys drank for England (with Ireland and Wales thrown in for good measure!) They always had a drink in their hand at any given time of the day. The drummer would start his day with a plate of dry cornflakes, to which he would add a liberal splash of neat vodka. Their van had a row of optics attached to the side wall in the sitting area, which had every spirit you could want. It always baffled me how they could stand, never mind perform in their permanent drunken state, but perform they did, and with great success. I wished I knew their formula, because they were always bringing gorgeous girls back to the digs at any time, day or night.

As we grew more popular in the area, so we were having more problems with Lee. Not for the first time a band member was being told how great he was by audiences, and Lee was starting to believe it. Lately he had started to mention that he was the main attraction in the band, and without him the band would be nothing. This had a very bad effect on the rest of us, and when he started to demand a bigger share of the wage packet, we realised that we didn't want to work with him anymore. As the days went by on that tour he seemed to be getting even worse with his demands.

On the night before the last gig the rest of the band held a meeting and decided it was time for him to go. It was agreed that we would tell him at the gig and me being the longest serving member, was voted to be the one to tell him.

We set up and laid out our props in the dressing room in a very quiet and nervy atmosphere. There was a sign above the door leading to the stage which read "if you sing and tell jokes, for fucks sake sing!"(A bad omen.)

As we sat in the lounge having a drink before the show, Lee noticed how quiet we were.

"What's up?" He asked.

"Oh, nothing, we are just a bit tired," I said.

"No, what's going on?" He demanded.

"Fuck it, tell him Brick" said Bobby.

To me this was not the right time or place, but the dice had been cast and we couldn't go back now.

"Can I have a word with you in private?" I asked and ushered him into a corner of the room. "We can't help noticing that you haven't been happy lately, and you don't seem to be part of the band anymore. You're giving us the impression that you don't need us and that you would be far better off on your own, so we have decided to let you do your own thing, and when we have found a replacement, you can start a solo career which I'm sure you've been thinking about." (Very diplomatically put I thought.) "There's no rush though, you can take as long as you like," I continued.

Lee looked at me for a moment and said quietly "Yeah, I've been turning it over in my mind for a while now." He grabbed my hand and shook it.

"Ok then, we'll work on that when we get home shall we?" I answered him, feeling quite relieved. I returned to the table to be bombarded with questions.

"How'd it go, what did he say," and so forth.

"He was alright about it," I assured them, "didn't seem too much bothered, so everything is okay."

By this time it was about fifteen minutes until ShowTime so we finished our drinks and headed for the dressing room.

A committee member stopped us on the way and asked if everything was ok. We said everything was fine and asked him why he asked the question.

"Well, yer singer fella just left out the door with two suitcases under his arms and a face like thunder."

We looked at each other and raced to the dressing room. Gone! He had taken most of the props and costume changes. Only a few were left, and those were the tatty ones we kept in reserve. The committee man had followed us in and demanded to know what was going on.

"The bastards done a runner and taken all our props," informed Bobby.

"Be that as it may bonny lads, but I've booked a comedy band and a comedy band I expect!" Came the answer. With no other option we frantically scribbled down a makeshift act on paper with the meagre materials that we had at hand and performed as best we could. Surprisingly, we went down pretty well and as the second spot was always a dance spot, we covered the rest of the night comfortably. We raced back to the digs to find Lee had packed his bags and gone.

We told Adam first thing in the morning as we prepared to journey home, and he got right on with the job of finding a replacement. It's funny how things fall into place sometimes, because, no sooner were we home when Adam phoned to say he had a replacement for Lee and so entered Johnny to our merry band.

This could not have worked out better for us, as Johnny was a very experienced singer who had worked with all the top bands in the Edinburgh area and was an excellent impersonator to boot.

After two weeks of intensive rehearsals we were ready to hit the road again. We had added some new impersonations to the act thanks to Johnny and the show was stronger than ever. the timing for the new act could not have come at a better time, as the money was running low in all our pockets. As the old saying goes, "no play, no pay."

Chapter Thirteen
They Shoot Horses Don't They?

Adam had been busy and had got us more "extra" work to ensure we had some money coming in. If we had a smooth transition with the new act being readied, he also worked a miracle to get Johnny an Equity card so he could join us. This time it was a period drama, set in central Scotland in nineteen-ten.

The scene called for an outside location in Fife. It was to be a coal miner's holiday, or "fair day" as they called it, with races, fun-fair, and picnics on the grass. We were ushered into wardrobe and fitted with cloth caps, itchy woollen shirts, britches and braces, and to top it all off, hobnail boots.

It was a big production and there were over one hundred of us "extras" all dressed in similar gear. The faces of the passersby were a picture as we trooped out of the studio to the buses waiting to take us to the site. They must have thought that they had been transported back in time. We hadn't been at the location for more than a few minutes when the director called us to him. Standing on a chair to be seen by everyone, he issued us our respective positions for the "shoot."

"About twenty of you go up and spread yourselves on that hill." He instructed, pointing at the area. "I'll need another twenty-two to be playing football directly below that," he added. "The rest of you just mill around in the shot and make like you are enjoying yourselves."

He was about to jump off the chair when he remembered something. "Has anyone worked with horses before?" He asked.

I suddenly found myself standing alone in front of him, as everyone else had dissolved into the background.

"Ahh, good man" he beamed.

"But I don't know anything about horses!" I told him.

"Good, good, just go over there and Nigel will explain what you have to do," he said, completely ignoring my protests.

A very bored Nigel took my arm and led me to a pony and trap waiting out of shot.

"Here's the script, the main scene is in front of you over there, and when the boss shouts action! You lead the pony across the shot in the background, got it?"

"But I don't know anything about horses." I repeated.

"Listen," he snarled, "it ain't fucking rocket science, all you have to do is lead that midget, flea-ridden nag across the shot, so just do it, we haven't got time to fuck about!"

Realising that I was wasting my time protesting, I went across to the pony, and gingerly picked up the reins. It looked up at me with tired, disinterested eyes and by way of introduction, urinated over my boots. There was no time to dry off as everyone was in position for the scene.

"Action!" Cried the director and everyone began acting out their roles. Nigel pointed to me to begin my "walk on" and I set off. One step later and I was yanked to an abrupt halt as the pony dug it's hooves in and refused to budge.

"Cut!" Yelled the director, "what's the problem?"

"It won't move," I said lamely.

"Well you're the horse fella, make it move!" He ordered.

Everyone took up their positions again.

"Action!" Yelled the director once more. This time the bloody horse backed up about three yards, tossing its head up and down and whinnying loudly.

"Cut!" Screamed the director. "What the fucks up now?"

"It won't do as it's told" I said.

"Well fucking tell it!" Nigel suggested that it might be frightened with all the lights and cameras, and maybe if I stroked its nose, it might help to calm it down a bit. I did as was suggested and was rewarded with a head butt under my chin which had me seeing stars, and nearly knocked me out. (I swear that the four-legged bastard was grinning at me).

"Come on people, time is ticking!" The director shouted impatiently, ignoring my swelling chin and eyeing me darkly.

Take three, and I was still wrestling with the damn pony.

"Look, you useless arsehole, I don't care how you get that fucking horse to move past the main scene, toss it off, set fire to its arse if you have to, but get it mobile!" Thundered the boss.

By this time the whole cast were eyeing me with daggers, with the exception of Charlie, Bobby, Freddie, and Johnny, who were doubled up in laughter. It was showdown time.

"Right you bastard, when I say move, you fucking move!" I hissed. To make my point I whacked it a mighty wallop on its nose. The pony whinnied in pain and its eyes took on a frightened look. (Come on people, it was tit for tat!)

Take four, and the scene went off without a hitch. I abandoned my four-footed friend as soon as I could and joined the rest of the band, who were still roaring with laughter at my little episode.

"That was priceless!" Giggled Freddie. "Lester Piggott you are not!"

"Don't come any nearer," said Johnny, holding his nose, "you stink like a piss house!"

After a few more scenes were shot we were told to make up a part of the crowd sitting on the hill, supposedly having a picnic. It had just started to drizzle with rain and the director, in a caring mood, had handed out sheets of clear plastic for us to sit on and keep our bottoms dry. It also kept the costumes dry and saved any lost Time filming having to have them dry cleaned (the real reason.)

Unfortunately, as the rain grew heavier, and the hill got wetter, we all began sliding down the hill as if we were on sleds. Admitting defeat, the boss broke for lunch to wait for the weather to improve. As we stood in line for our food we were handed a paper plate each to eat from. The rain got worse and came down relentlessly and in no time, our plates were reduced to a soggy pulp, drooping limply around our hands. To make matters worse, the pony was led past us under the protection of an oversized umbrella to be fed its hay first. As I stood there in the queue, with water streaming down the back of my neck, I had never hated an animal so much in all my life.

The weather proved too bad and after a watery lunch we were given the rest of the day off and boarded the bus for home. The following morning we arrived on the site to be told that the pony had died in the night and that the scene would have to be shot all over again.

With the director calling for the "horse fella" from yesterday I quickly hid myself in a large group of extras and waited until they finally picked someone else for the job. Our next task was to stage a football game, where the main character was to score a goal. Simple enough you might think.

Unfortunately the main character was totally miscast in my opinion, as he would probably prefer to have his nails done and eyebrows plucked. I had grave doubts he had ever seen a football never mind kick the damn thing. Time after time, when it came to the crucial time for him to score, he would miss the ball completely, or tap it so weakly, that it wouldn't convince anyone he knew anything about the game.

After fifteen "takes" we, the extras, who had been doing all the running around, were at the exhausted stage. Finally, in answer to our prayers, our champion kicked a perfect shot and as it flew into the top corner of the net, the goalkeeper pulled off a save that would have been admired by the professionals. His look of triumph changed to shock when he realised what he had done.

"Oh heck, oh fuck!" He stammered, as the rest of us gave him withering looks, "it was instinct honest!" He pleaded.

The goalie joined the pony on my "most hated" list.

There was a real character in our group of extras called Happy Howden. Happy was the original "blue" comic in Scotland. Very funny but downright filthy. One of the stories about him (and there were many,) was of his engagement to do a spot at a highly prestigious civic meeting. All the top dignitaries were there, and when Happy arrived, one of them recognised him and realising that someone had made an almighty cock up, bundled him into a toilet.

"Look Happy," he said. "I don't know who booked you but your act definitely won't go down well with this type of crowd, is there any way you could clean it up a bit?"

Happy looked hurt and said, "but I'm renowned as blue comic, dirty jokes, bad language, that's what I'm all about."

"Please Happy," the man pleaded, "just try it clean this one time for me."

"Okay," said Happy, "I'll do my best."

As he strolled onto the stage that night, faced with an audience donned in dinner suits and evening gowns, Happy looked down at the poor guy who had approached him and gave him a reassuring wink. Grabbing the microphone, he began his act.

"Ladies and gentlemen, it is indeed a privilege and pleasure to be present in front of you tonight. As you may, or may not know, I am regarded as a blue comedian, and have often offended people with the language I use. However, tonight, as I am in the presence of such distinguished guests, I will replace any said swear words I may use in my act with the word cabbage. So, there was this fucking great cabbage!" He told us that it was one of the shortest performances he ever did.

Another story concerning him was when he was booked to appear at a catholic club in Glasgow. On arriving, he was told that someone had somehow managed to walk into the club in the afternoon that day when it was really busy and make off with the brand-new television from the lounge. Happy shook his head, tutted in sympathy and got ready to go on. As he walked on to the stage, he noticed a life-sized wooden carving of Jesus on the cross fixed to the back wall of the stage.

"I see you got the bastard who pinched your telly!" He said. (Another short spot and a police escort from the club to boot!)

Anyway, Happy was in our group of extras and was always ready to get his face in front of the cameras. This proved his downfall, as he appeared a little too often in the shots. The final straw was when we filmed a race scene. It was shot in three stages. The start, a shot of the runners about half way running flat out, and the end of the race where our hero bursts the tape with his chest to win.

At the playback of the scene, there was Happy at the start, shouting words of encouragement to our lad. He was there again at the half way stage as the hero ran past him in full flight, and when he wins the race, Happy is the first to meet and congratulate him. This caused the director to have a raging fit and he banished Happy from all other filming on the set, but seeing how he kept the other extras spirits up with his wisecracks, he was allowed to stay on full pay, with the strict instruction that he didn't go within forty yards of any cameras.

Happy was not one to bother with the intricacies of the tax laws of the land, and it was no surprise, when a few years later, he was called in to the Inland Revenue's office to explain his lack of payments to her majesty's government. He learned to his cost that the tax offices take no prisoners when monies were owed to them. After a few futile attempts to pacify them, they took his bank balance, his home, and his car. Furious, he stormed into the office and said, "you've got everything else, you may as well take this too!"

With that he whipped off his toupee and threw it on the counter. From that day on Happy worked the clubs as bald as a coot.

Chapter Fourteen
A Welcome in the Hillsides

The filming of that periodical drama took two weeks to complete and in between filming, Adam had organised a couple of gigs locally to settle the new act in. At the first one an indignant committee member asked if he could say a few words to the audience before we started.

"Ladies and gentlemen," he announced over the microphone, "it has come to my attention that certain allegations have been made against this committee regarding the money raised for the new billiards room. One of these allegations is that not all of the money raised has gone into this project, and that some of the cash has ended up in our pockets. Let me tell you right now that these allegations are totally unfounded, and when we find the alligators responsible for these rumours, they will be banned from this club for life!"

He didn't seem to notice the audience doubled up in hysterics at his gaff.

A trip to Wales was next on the calendar and our base would be Newport, Gwent. From there it would be central for all the clubs in the coal mining villages in the valleys of South Wales. It was a hard life for these people, with many of their village landscapes scarred by the pits that gave them their livelihood.

However, as is the case with most people in these circumstances, their sense of humour shone through. It was weird, but in almost every club we played there the committees took great pleasure telling us how they once paid the great Tom Jones off, because he was no good. I kept thinking, if he was that bad, how the hell did he rise to the superstar status that he did.

For me, a Welshman has only three priorities in his life. Rugby, drinking and rugby again. Almost every male that had matured beyond the embryo stage of his life will have travelled to Murreyfield in Edinburgh for the international match there. This would happen every two years and as soon as it was over, they would start saving up for the next trip.

Over the years they had formed an affectionate bond with the Scots who always made them welcome. Being Scots, this made our tour so much easier, as the English acts were definitely treated with less enthusiasm. An instance of this bond between nations takes me back to a few years earlier, when walking down the Main Street in Musselburgh. I noticed this little guy bedecked in the red scarf of Wales, and carrying a huge plastic leek under his arm, staggering along the road.

Considering the match had been played almost two weeks earlier, I asked him why he was still here.

"Well boyo" he answered in his Welsh

lilt, "I promised myself that I wasn't going home till I spent all my money see, but every time I goes into a pub, you Scots buggers insist on buying me drinks!"

The Welsh girls are very pretty and also very friendly. We had an arrangement with our landlord who was single, that if we came back to the digs with girls, they could stay as long as we paid for their breakfasts, and maybe bring a girl back for him as well.

About a week into the tour I was walking through the shopping centre in Newport when I passed a shop which was obviously open, but had brown paper pasted over all its windows and doors. As I peeked inside I saw it was full of sex toys, rubber dolls, and "porn" magazines. I had never been in a sex shop before and it must have shown on my face, as the assistant behind the counter gave me a "here's a right naïve arsehole" look.

"You looking or buying?" he snapped.

"Oh, I'm just browsing."

"Well don't be flicking through the magazines unless you intend to buy them," he ordered. After a few minutes looking around, I bought a cheap vibrator, thinking of having some fun with the lovely lass I had arranged to meet that night.

Back at the digs after the show I tried out my new purchase on the lady in question, and we both agreed that it was money well spent.

At breakfast the next morning Freddie asked me about the peculiar buzzing noise coming from my room in the middle of the night.

"That will be the vibrator I bought yesterday!" I replied.

"You dirty bugger! Where did you get that from?" He asked.

"There's a sex shop in the town centre." I explained. He asked if I could get one for him, and I said I would if I was passing. News like that doesn't take long to get around and before I knew it, everybody in the band, including the roadie, were pleading me to get them one as well.

The following day saw me trooping back to the shop. As I entered I was met by a hostile stare from the assistant.

"We don't give refunds, if that vibrator's been used and it's broke, then it's your hard luck!" He snapped.

"No, I want to buy five more."

He looked at me in disgust. "I've had some really sick bastards come in here, but you take the fucking biscuit!" He sneered. I immediately put him right, telling him that they were for friends.

"Thank fuck for that, I had horrible visions of you sticking them up her arse, and yours as well, while you were on the job." It was my turn to look disgusted as I hurriedly paid and left the shop.

That night we were up in the valleys, playing in a club near Mountain Ash. It was on such a steep incline and the track was so bad, that we had to carry all the equipment up the last hundred yards. We had plenty of help from the locals but even so lugging six and a half tons of gear up a hill didn't put us in the best moods for the show.

But, as with everything else when you are on the road, you just have to grin and bear it. With the gear up and the sound checked I found I really needed to go to the toilet, so I asked the barman where they were.

"Is it a number one or a number two that you want?" He asked. I looked puzzled, so he asked me again. "Do you want a piss or a shit?"

I looked around me in embarrassment and whispered that I needed a "number two."

"Well, you'll find the doors stacked up by the side of the fruit machine and the toilets are just through the door on the left."

"Doors, what doors?" I asked.

"The doors for the toilets!" He said in exasperation. I looked puzzled. "Listen," he explained, "every second Saturday we have a home game with our rugby team see, and as often as not, seeing as how they are a bag of shit they gets beat, so, when they comes into the club after the game, they takes their frustration out on the toilet doors, kicking them off their hinges they do, so that's why, every second Saturday, I takes the doors off, and puts them back on Sunday morning, see."

Having had this explained to me I could see the logic in it, but it didn't take away the embarrassing fact that everyone in the club would know where I was going and what I would be doing there.

The call of nature was too strong for me to delay my visit to a later time, so I pushed my way through the packed bar and picked up my door. This gave rise to a few obvious comments from the crowd, such as "going for a shit are we?"

I nodded my head lamely and headed for the toilets, all the while being followed by a little guy who had befriended me, telling me what a great singer his brother was. "He's even better than Tom Jones, he is" he remarked. "Mind you, we've had Tom Jones here, paid him off we did," he added smugly. (Another venue our Tom can't go back to.) He kept up this non-stop chatter all the way to the toilets, oblivious to my struggle manipulating the damn door past hordes of people milling around supping pints. By the time I had reached the toilet, and hurriedly jammed the door in the vacant space, my bowels felt as though they were going to explode.

"Sorry to ignore you, but I'm a bit desperate" I said from the sanctuary of my little cubicle.

"Don't you bother, boyo" he said, as he popped his head over the cubicle next to mine, staring down at me with my trousers at my ankles. "Anyway, as I was saying," and he carried on his conversation from where he left off. This, I thought, made the effort with that fucking door a totally useless exercise.

With the show over, and with what little dignity I had left, we headed back to Newport. The show had gone really well and we had a few eager young girls accompanying us home (for tea and biscuits of course.)

With plenty of beer and spirits at hand, the party soon got into full swing. After a few hours everyone began pairing off and headed to their rooms. Soon after, a buzzing noise could be heard coming from every room, with groans of pleasure echoing along the hallway. The only room that was "buzz free "was mine. The damn batteries had run out!

We had just returned home when Adam booked us for another ten-day run in Wales again. (Bad organization.) This time however, we would be playing an American Air Base on the way there. This was where Johnny was a godsend to us, as he had worked in American Air Bases in Turkey and knew what was required to go down well with their audiences.

Three days of intensive rehearsals to take the "Britishness" out of the act, add a few classic American rock numbers and we were as ready as we could be in the short time that had been available.

The base was in Suffolk and was an ex R.A.F. aerodrome. As soon as we entered the gates it was as if we were in America. The noises, the smells, (even the toilets had American detergents!) were totally alien to us.

Thank god Johnny had educated us to their humour and music tastes. With our newly gained knowledge we gave them a show they really appreciated and went down a storm. After the show two very pretty girl soldiers paid particular attention to Freddie and myself and asked us back to their room for a "drink."

The room was pretty basic, with a toilet, some cupboards, and a double bunk bed in the corner. I noticed that on the bottom bunk there was a hand rail fitted. I presumed it was there for the occupant to do some "pull up" exercises. No sooner had we been given a drink when the girls adjourned to the toilet to come back seconds later, wearing matching flimsy negligees. Freddie's girl took his hand, and led him to the bottom bunk, where she peeled off her nightwear to reveal a stunning body.

"Well. That'll do for me," said Freddie, and stripped naked beside her. Within a minute he was straddling her and doing "the business." As he thrust merrily away, his date raised her feet and rested them on the hand rail above her bunk. It was obvious that this was not the first time she had done this.

Seeing all this going on, my date in the meantime had shed her nightwear, and was unzipping my jeans ready for her piece of the action. For some reason, warning bells were ringing in my head and, much as I was just as eager to copy Freddie's gymnastics, something was holding me back.

"Sorry, I really like you but I think I've caught an infection, and I couldn't forgive myself if I passed it on to you," I said.

This, I thought, would kill off any sexual desire my partner had. "That's ok, we'll just use a condom, and anyway we have quite a few cures for that sort of thing "she said, not in the slightest put off.

"Listen, I'm married." I said.

"So what, so am I, let's get cosy!" She answered, tugging at my shirt and jeans, urgently trying to get me undressed.

"No, sorry" I apologised again, "I don't think I can do this." I stood up and pulled up my jeans, stuffing my shirt in at the same time.

"You're a fag, ain't ya?" she yelled.

"No, no, I just don't feel right about it," I explained.

"You've been wasting my time you bum fucker! Why didn't you tell me you were gay!" She screamed. While all this was going on, Freddie and his partner were busily sawing away oblivious to the heated row that was going on in the room. Realising that to stay any longer would only make matters worse, I brushed past my frustrated date into the night and back to the digs, all the while wondering to myself why I had passed up a sure-fire certainty.

The next morning at breakfast Freddie came down with a grin like a Cheshire cat on his face.

"What happened to you last night?" He asked. I made some lame excuse about not feeling too well.

"Well you missed out big time there chum, shagged the pair of them, what a couple of goers!" He smirked. After breakfast we headed down from Suffolk to Newport and began our tour.

Four days in, and Freddie had become very quiet, not his usual bubbly self. As we sat in the digs lounge on our own one afternoon, he motioned me over to him.

"You know them two Yankee birds," he whispered.

"Yeah, what about them?" I asked.

"Well, I think I've caught something off them."

I burst out laughing, "I knew it, I knew it!" I chortled, "I knew it in my bones that something was not quite right there."

"Keep your voice down," he hissed, "I'm gonna have to go to the doctors and get it sorted, will you come with me?"

"Me! Why me!" I said.

"Cos' if you hadn't fucked off and left me, you might have got the one with the clap!" (A bit of a strange and selfish logic I thought.)

Fifteen minutes later saw us at the nearest doctor's surgery waiting patiently to be seen. After thirty minutes Freddie had been examined and instructed to go to the other side of town where they had the facilities to treat sexual diseases.

On arrival, a bored looking receptionist informed us that it was ladies day and to come back in the morning.

"Sorry, but we won't be here in the morning," said Freddie.

"Why, where will you be?" she snapped.

"Well, I'm part of a travelling cabaret show and we are heading for Swansea after tonight's show." Said Freddie.

She gave him a withering look and told him to take a seat for a minute while she consulted the doctor on duty.

She returned soon after to tell Freddie he would see him. "Go through the door on your left, pass the first waiting room carry on through the double doors, and take a seat in the next waiting area and the doctor will be with you shortly," she informed him, handing him a piece of paper with a number on it. As we passed the first waiting room, which was full of women, Freddie grinned and said "well, we know who not to go shagging with the next time we are here."

On to the second room which was completely empty, with only rows and rows of empty chairs filling the space. We had been sitting for only a few minutes when we heard footsteps approaching, and a little Asian guy with a white coat and stethoscope round his neck popped his head around the screen curtain in front of us.

"Number seven, three, six, two, five, please!" He hollered. I found this really funny, considering the room was empty apart from Freddie and myself, and he was the only one with the relevant paper in his hand.

Freddie jumped up no shouted "bingo!" and headed behind the screen. His attempt at humour did not go down well with the doctor, who gave him a similar look the receptionist had given him.

"Name please?" I heard him ask.

Freddie told him his full name. "Address?"

Freddie told him his address. "Ah, so you are Scottish, yes?" He asked in a heavy accent. Freddie confirmed this.

"So, what seems to be the problem?" The doctor asked. "Well, I've got a bit of a discharge down below," explained Freddie. The doctor ordered him to drop his pants for an inspection. A minute or so of a few "hmms" and "aahs" from the doctor behind the screen, and the examination seemed to be over. All the while, I sat in my chair at the front, listening to their conversation.

"I'm going to take a test sample, and it may sting a little," said the doc.

"Aaaaaargh! Fucking hell!" Screamed Freddie. I sat in my chair, shoulders heaving in silent laughter at Freddie's discomfort.

"Now the lady in question, what was her name?" The good doctor asked.

"Dunno" said Freddie, "she was an American, I didn't get her name, it was a one night stand."

"And where did you meet this lady?" The doc continued icily.

"It was on an air force base in Suffolk." Freddie answered. The doctor suddenly yanked back the screen and threw the clipboard he had been carrying to the ground and screamed.

"Good bloody god in heaven, we have a Scotsman, screwing an American, in England, coming to a Welsh clap clinic, to be treated by a Pakistani doctor! What the bloody hell chance have we of containing these diseases!" He picked up his clipboard, scribbled something on his prescription pad, threw it at me and stormed out of the room.

By this time I was on the floor, doubled up in laughter with tears running down my cheeks. Freddie appeared from behind the screen, wincing with pain and doing a fair impression of a John Wayne walk.

"The bastard near ripped my cock off!" He moaned.

"C'mon," I said, "let's get your tablets and go home."

Chapter Fifteen
See Naples and Die

We returned to Scotland to find Adam was giving up the agency, but his brother Eddie was now going to handle our affairs. This did not bother us as he had been involved quite heavily in our management over the last few months.

Our gigs for the Americans had gone down so well in England, that their entertainments team had arranged a mini tour of Italy, Germany, and Belgium, so once again, we headed south to Felixstowe to catch the night channel ferry. (Why was it always the night ferry?)

We only had three days to get to Naples in the south of Italy from Edinburgh, and with our tired old Transit van struggling to reach its maximum of fifty to fifty-five miles per hour, we realised that we would have to drive non-stop through the night to get there on time. Against all odds our trusty old van (which was making some alarming knocking noises under the bonnet by now) rolled up to the gates of the NATO base in Naples three days later.

An American soldier on sentry duty eyed our unkempt, unshaven bodies with suspicion and asked for identification. Having satisfied his screening, he asked us in a rich southern drawl what time our flight had come in. When we told him that we had driven all the way from Scotland, he looked in amazement at us.

"In that?" He shouted incredulously, pointing to our poor old van. When we confirmed that we had, he just shook his head in disbelief and lifted the barrier. After that epic journey we were tired and smelly but we only just had time to set up the gear, grab a quick shower in the hotel and get back for the show.

When we had left an hour earlier the hall had been laid out with tables and chairs over the whole area, but on our return, a partition over seven-foot high had been erected down the middle, which effectively split the hall in two, and one side of it now had long rows of benches running down it. When I asked why this had been done, I was told that a Martin Luther King revival group had booked half the room at the last minute.

As usual with my luck, the revival section was on my side of the room. The fact that a five piece band was going to be blasting out loud music while they were holding their prayers had totally escaped the organisers.

The evening went as bad as I thought it would, with the rest of the band receiving an enthusiastic reception, while I, on the other side of the "wall" was met by icy stares and furious gestures to leave the stage. Back at the hotel, while the rest of the band, fired up on adrenaline, and in high spirits, were in a party mood, I slunk off to bed.

It was about lunchtime when we all met up to explore our surroundings. Our romantic notion of Naples were soon dispelled, with the hotel receptionist advising us not to venture out in the streets alone as we would be easy targets for the muggers which were rife in the city.

Our hotel was in a less auspicious part of the city with an avenue of trees spaced about twenty-metres apart. Leaning against each tree was a prostitute plying her trade. Cars would drive slowly up and down, stop at the lady of their choice, they would haggle noisily over the cost and when the price was agreed, the girl would jump in the car and off they would go. When the "deed" was done, she would be brought back to lean on her tree and wait for the next customer.

The busiest of all the girls by far was a much older woman, who must have been in her sixties by her appearance. She was never standing by her tree for more than five minutes, day or night, before a car would stop and pick her up. Intrigued, I asked the hotel manager why she was so popular.

"Ah meester Brick eet ees because she gives, how you say, "blow job" but take teeth out!"

"Eet is much like real thing, but no bad diseases, yes?"

Because of the dangerous location of our

accommodation we spent the remaining two days cooped up in the hotel, venturing out only to do the gigs we had been booked for. The old saying "see Naples and die" had a very ironic ring to it.

As we drove out of the city, heading for Pisa, there was a quiet sense of relief amongst us. We journeyed north, bypassing Monte Cassino where there had been bitter fighting during the Second World War, past Rome, as we had on good information been told not to drive in the city as a tourist, as the locals were better known for aiming their cars rather than driving them. We finally arrived in Pisa with a day to spare.

This was a rare treat for us. Usually there was very little time between gigs, so Johnny and I decided to make the most of it and visit the famous leaning tower. Sure enough, there it was in all its glory, gleaming white and leaning alarmingly. After a few photo's we spotted a café across the way and went in for some refreshment. When we staggered out a few hours later we both swore blind that the damn tower was as straight as a die.

Pisa was another good gig for us (me included this time!) And we had three days before our next gig in Germany, so we could take our time and nurse the old van up the "boot of Italy." We stopped to fill the tank at a little service station at the side of the road and I noticed they were selling two-litre bottles of the local wine at a ridiculously low price. Always one for a bargain I bought three bottles. I was even more pleased with myself, as I had haggled with the attendant and got the lot for the price of three coffees. The fact that there were foreign bits of things floating around in the bottles didn't deter me in the least.

"Anyone for some vino?" I asked, settling down in the back of the van. The others eyed my wine with suspicion and declined my offer.

"Suit yourselves, all the more for me!" I said as I uncorked the first bottle. I was surprised how crisp and light it tasted, and with a big smile on my face made myself even more comfortable and poured another large glassful.

I woke up feeling as though someone was hammering six-inch nails into my skull, with a tongue like sandpaper and broken glass behind my eyes. The empty wine bottles were lolling around with the movement of the van.

"Are we in Austria yet?" I asked.

"Nope" came Johnny's clipped reply.

"When do you think we'll get there?" I asked once more.

"Passed through it yesterday!" Freddie snapped.

"So we're in Germany then?" I persisted.

"Yeh, and you've missed two days, you drunken bastard!"

"I didn't do anything stupid did I?" I asked sheepishly.

"Oooh no!" replied Johnny, "you only decided you needed a piss just as we had reached the highest point on the road over the alps, jumped out when we were moving, and nearly fell down the fucking mountain, you stupid prick!" I made a silent note to myself, never to buy wine that didn't have a label on it, ever again.

The gig in Germany was at the Frankfurt Rhine-Maine air base. It was spread over a massive area with thousands of American military personnel there. The first thing we noticed after going through the gates was the lack of white faces on the base. In fact, as we drove down the road towards the G.I. club where we were playing, it seemed as though we were the only white faces there.

As we set up and sound checked a few black guys came over to ask what kind of music we played. We told them we did a cabaret show, and then a rock set as a musical finale.

"Shit! You gotta be yanking our chain man!" One of them said. "Take a look around boy, you see any rednecks here, this club is ours this is soul and disco land, we don't want no rock shit here!"

With that they walked off, shaking their heads and laughing to themselves.

His words rang true on that night, as we went down like a lead balloon with the audience and were politely told to "take the rest of the night off," after the first set. The major in charge came over to us to apologise, telling us we had been booked into the wrong club and promising to give the person responsible a piece of his mind, but that didn't make us feel any better as we were not used to failure.

With our tails between our legs we set off the next morning to our final gig on the Belgian border. We were relieved to see the crowd there were mainly white and a more mature age (in their thirties.) After a storming reception at the end of the show our confidence was back at a peak and a good night was had by all. In the morning we boarded our trusty (rusty) old van and set off for the channel ferry at Zeebrugge and home.

We had nursed the engine all the way to Italy and back, but by this time it was making some alarming grinding noises. As we drove along, bypassing Brussels, Bobby told me to get the foot down or we would miss the ferry. (I'm driving again.)

"I'm taking it easy so I won't knacker the engine," I shouted above the noise of the sick engine.

"Listen, if it was going to fuck up it would have done it by now, trust me, I used to be a mechanic!" Said Bobby.

With this expert advice given to me I eased the throttle pedal down to give us our maximum of fifty-five miles per hour.

Less than five minutes later a horrible clattering noise, followed by a bang, came from under the bonnet and we trundled to a halt in the breakdown lane.

"Wassup?" everyone shouted, roused from their sleep.

"The engine's packed in!" I told them.

"You haven't been gunning it have you?" Asked Johnny. I told them that Bobby, being a mechanic and all, had given me the go ahead to speed up.

"Mechanic! That fat bastard couldn't change a fucking tyre!" He raged. Bobby by this time was conspicuous by his absence having disappeared for a pee. Everyone gathered around the stricken engine (with the exception of our expert mechanic) and tapped a few things with spanners, but it was plain to see there was something seriously wrong.

After a few minutes I decided that the emergency services were going to be required, and set off to find an emergency roadside phone. (There were no mobiles in those days.) After half a mile or so I found one and passed on our whereabouts to an operator who spoke good English.

By the time I had walked back to the van there was a little fellow in greasy overalls with his head buried under the bonnet, banging away and muttering to himself in Belgique. He emerged and asked in bad English, "the engeene, she go brrrrring, yes?"

I said that was the exact noise.

"Ah, then 'tis fucked!" He said, shaking his head sadly. Everyone turned to Bobby, looking daggers at him. Through limited verbal communication and sign language, he explained that he would have to take us to Ostend and not Zeebrugge as his base was there. From there our van would be put on the ferry to Dover where the recovery team in Britain would take over.

After a hair-raising journey where our little mechanic drove at breakneck speed with no thought for the terrified passengers sitting in the knackered van attached to the rear of his truck, we arrived in Ostend. The paperwork was completed in record time and we were treated to the spectacle of four of the oldest inhabitants of the town (average age about ninety!) Helping our mechanic push our three-ton van onto the cross-channel ferry.

We spent a relaxing few hours in the bar during our crossing before docking in Dover. Back on home soil, the British red tape system came into play.

No, we weren't allowed to push our van off the ferry, no, we would have to wait for a tow unit (when they could find one.)

We were eventually taken off the boat by a very disgruntled driver, complaining loudly about missing his tea break (welcome home!)

Abandoned in the car park, we were left

to our own means waiting for the relay service to come to our aid. Four hours later a little five hundred weight van pulled up beside us.

"What's up with the van?" Our bored saviour asked.

"Engines packed up!" Replied Johnny.

"Won't go then eh? he continued. I began to have serious doubts about his mechanical skills, and said sarcastically, "didn't take you long to sort that out."

This fell on deaf ears. "Shame that, my vans too small to tow that heavy brute, I'll have to phone head office to send something bigger." And with that, he bade us a cheery farewell and drove off. Considering we had told the recovery service the size and weight of our van as soon as we had docked, this left everyone with serious doubts about the efficiency of the service.

After another four-hour wait a vehicle that could do the job finally appeared. The driver told us he could only take us to London, where we would be transferred to the next unit. (It appeared they only operated in certain areas and would have to transfer at each one.)

So began a nightmare journey from Dover to London, London to Bristol, Bristol to Birmingham, Birmingham to Manchester, Manchester to Carlisle, and finally, Carlisle to Edinburgh. It had taken over fifty hours from the time we had broken down until I wearily turned the key in the lock of my front door.

Numb with exhaustion I was met by a very angry wife who would not listen to the reason for my delay and had decided that I must have been having a great time. This did nothing to improve my already foul mood, and a blazing row ensued. (Welcome home again!)

Chapter Sixteen
The Dark Continent

A few days later saw us involved in more extras work. The TV play we were to take part in was a period drama about the first woman doctor in Scotland and her struggle to be accepted in the male dominated medical profession.

Our roles were to be male medical students, barring her way at the entrance of the university on her first day there. Being set in Victorian times, we were all grandly dressed in frock coats and top hats. On the day of the "shoot" we were grouped around the entrance of the old university gates, and as usual it was pouring with rain. There were the usual delays while the sound and lighting were adjusted and as usual, we were soaked to the skin by the time everything was ready.

The script required the main character to walk around the corner to be met by us angry students loudly voicing our disapproval at her being there.

After the first "take" the director was not satisfied with the amount of resentment we were showing.

"Why don't you all burst into a rousing song, say 'John Brown's Body' as she appears?" he suggested. We positioned our sodden bodies for the second take. As she rounded the corner, we broke into song with great gusto.

Unfortunately, most of the extras were singers in their own rite, or had something to do with the music business, and what was meant to be a vocal rabble turned out a harmonic rendition worthy of any choir.

"Stop!, stop!" Screamed the director. "What the hell are you all doing?" He demanded.

When we explained, he reverted back to the original plan. Take three saw the male hero of the play jump to the defence of the poor harassed woman as one of the extras was to push forward towards her in a threatening manner. The script required him to bar the way of the said aggressor and say, "one more step sir and I will knock the teeth from your head."

Unfortunately for the director, the man he had picked to be the threatening male was part of a comedy duo and was known for being a little crazy. Our hero delivered his line.

"One more step sir and I will knock the teeth from your head," whereupon our evil villain spat out his full set of false teeth into his open palm and offered them up to him. The entire cast fell about in fits of laughter (with the exception of the director.) Take four saw our toothless friend replaced with another villain, and the scene went to plan.

The final scene was to be a heated verbal confrontation between us students and our hero, with comments such as "she shall not pass these hallowed gates" and "you are an abomination sir, to sanction the passage of a woman into these corridors."

While this was going on, the rain was pouring down incessantly. This proved too much for our toothless villain, who pushed his way to the front of the baying mob and said, "Fuck it! I'm piss wet through, let the bitch in!" (Exit one toothless extra with the director tearing his hair out and screaming for blood.)

We had a meeting with Eddie later that week. "How would you like a trip to South Africa?" he said.

Apparently, a South African agent in charge of the Holiday Inn circuit over there had caught our show by chance and liked what he saw.

"Don't they have apartheid over there?" Charlie asked. (For those of you too young to remember, apartheid was a segregation law run by the white South African community to rule over the majority black population.)

"Yes, but the Holiday Inns over there run a no colour bar rule, because it's part of an American chain." Eddie explained.

"How long will we be going for?" I asked. Eddie said that it would be for a few weeks. The money was going to be some of the best we had ever earned, with food, accommodation, and all travel expenses covered. A meeting was arranged with the South African agent and all the details, such as work permits, flights, equipment, were ironed out. We would leave at the end of April, which left us a few weeks to work our contracts out in the U.K.

Bobby had started to get the "I am the band" syndrome, and was becoming a real diva. My relationship with him had deteriorated over the past year and I had begun to dislike him intensely. His selfishness and arrogance had started to irritate me to the point where the less I saw of him the better.

He, on the other hand, took my cool approach to him as regarding him inferior to me, and disliked me just as much. This state of affairs was to go on for a further two decades. The rest of the band seemed to be able to put up with his nonsense with the exception of Johnny. He disliked him even more than me.

"Who does that little fat bastard think he is?" He said as we sat having a drink one night. "He's only funny cos' he looks the part, and all his comedy ideas are ones he has pinched off other acts."

I had to agree with him on that.

"I tell you Brick, I can't take much more of that big mouthed thick cunt, and I'm gonna smack him shortly if he doesn't stop acting as though he owns the band."

The threat was carried out much quicker than expected, as the next night, Bobby was even more obnoxious than usual, bragging how great he was and how much the band depended on him. (In front of a gullible crowd as usual.)

This tipped Johnny over the edge. Without a word, he raised himself slowly out of his chair and went over to a fire point, lifted a fire extinguisher from its cradle, walked over to Bobby, and whacked him over the head with it. (knocking him out cold in mid brag.) He inspected it carefully for any damage and replaced it back on its rack.

"There, that should shut the fat twat up for a bit!" He told the stunned crowd.

Johnny casually drained his pint glass and ambled out of the room.

Needless to say, this did nothing to improve the relationship between the two of them and it started to affect the show. Johnny, being a professional, would carry on as usual, while Bobby would try to mess up his parts.

This made me realise just how stupid he was, as this could only affect the act overall. The crunch came swiftly. We were in Wales again for a week's run and Johnny had been unusually quiet, staying in his room whenever we were not working.

"I tell you Brick, I can't stand being in the same country, never mind the same room as that bastard," he told me over breakfast one morning. I tried to make things easier for him, by hinting that we could maybe get rid of him in the near future, but he just shook his head.

"Nah, the rest of the guys wouldn't go for that," he said. That was the last time I ever saw him. When I went to his room that night to call him to get ready for the gig, he was gone. Once again we had to come up with a makeshift act to get us through the night and somehow we pulled it off again.

Back at the digs, we sat in the lounge, discussing what we would do next. While we were talking about our problem we suddenly heard a groan from behind one of the couches. A hand appeared clutching a half-empty bottle of brandy, followed by a very intoxicated head. This was our first introduction to Gordon.

Gordon actually lived locally to me in Scotland, but had travelled professionally with bands almost since leaving school, so, although I knew him, it was only from a distance.

"Is that right you guys are looking for a singer?" He slurred. We told him we were looking for someone who could do impersonations as well.

"I can do that," he said. I had my doubts whether he could stand up, never mind impersonate at that moment.

"What about your own band?" Charlie asked.

"Packing up next week." He replied as he staggered to his feet and slumped down on to the couch next to us.

"So you're looking for a singer then?" He repeated. We did our best to humour him in his inebriated state and promised him an audition the next day, leaving him to sleep it off on the couch.

The next morning, to my surprise, there was Gordon sitting at the breakfast table, looking as fresh as a daisy.

"When are we doing the audition?" He asked. God! He may have been drunk, but his mind was as sharp as a tack. We had an impromptu rehearsal in his room, and even with no backing we could tell he was good. The props were brought out and amazingly, they fitted him perfectly. His impersonations were just as good. We couldn't believe our luck. I hurriedly phoned Eddie, who had been frantically searching for a replacement, to tell him the good news.

"Where did you find this guy?" He asked.

"Behind a couch." I replied. The phone went dead.

Although I was excited about the coming trip, there was a little matter of telling my wife. I knew that if I told her I was going to be gone for some time, she might not be happy, so I lied and said we were probably only away for a couple of weeks. I got the usual "go and enjoy yourself while I'm stuck here with the kids," routine, while I answered with the "well, the money's good," reply and we both left it at that.

Waiting at Edinburgh airport to catch our

flight I was struggling with mixed emotions. On the one hand I was excited about the new adventure we were about to take and on the other, sad to be apart from the kids. The icy stare from my better half helped to push the sad thoughts to the back of my mind as I boarded the plane.

The flight was with a Belgian airline called Sabina airways, which explained our first stop of the journey landing at Brussels airport. A two hour wait and then on to The Ivory Coast.

Here we had an hour to stretch our legs and get some refreshments. As soon as we exited the plane the stifling heat hit us even though it was late in the evening. I treated myself to a bottle of the local "Simba" beer and regretted it very soon after as I spent the next two flying hours camped in the plane's toilet

A few more hours later, and we arrived in Johannesburg. The agent was there to greet us and ushered us through to the departure lounge for the final stage of our journey to Cape Town on the southern tip of the country. There we were met by the hotel bus and driven back to meet the manager. The journey from Edinburgh to Cape Town had taken nearly twenty-four hours and we were absolutely exhausted, but this seemed to be overlooked by our new boss who wasted no time showing us our venue, what equipment was there, and all the timetable details we would need to adhere to.

"You look a little tired," he said finally, after two hours of being shown this and informed about that. "You'd better get your heads down so you can get yourselves ready for the first show tomorrow night," he said. (No rest for the wicked.) We were each given an en-suite double room in the hotel with a view looking over the harbour. I sat on my king-sized comfy bed.

Privacy! luxury! Not bad for a lad from a Musselburgh housing estate. My head hit the pillow and I slept the sleep of the totally exhausted for the next twelve hours.

The next day was frantically filled with collecting equipment from various music shops around the town and sound checking it back at the venue.

The place was called "Samantha's" and it was on the ground floor of the hotel. It boasted air conditioning (a new-fangled gadget to us Scots lads.)

It may have had it in the concert room, but it certainly didn't have it on the stage. Within five minutes of our opening show the sweat was pouring down our faces and large damp patches appeared on our stage suits. The show went down a storm with customers, management, and staff, gathering round us at the end to congratulate us, but with the heat and the long journey taking its toll, we declined the offer of drinks and uncharacteristically staggered off to bed.

After another good night's sleep in my luxurious room and a hearty breakfast in the dining room, I was ready to spend the day exploring Cape Town. It was a lovely place, with a vibrant harbour area and bustling streets, with an imposing view of Table Mountain overlooking it all. Add to this, the warm climate compared to the chilly winds of Scotland which I had just left, and this made me all the more excited about my new surroundings.

Later, we spent an hour or so in the cabaret room fine-tuning the sound system and adjusting the drum and guitar balances and were ready for the evening show. Our contract was for six shows per week from Monday to Saturday with every Sunday off. To know that we had a guaranteed day off was the icing on the cake for us, as we could make plans in advance to organise our free time.

Saturday night came and that first week had been very successful. Cape Town wasn't a big place then, and word had gotten around the town about us. Samantha's had been packed to capacity every night and with a five rand cover charge on the door, had made good money for the hotel.

The only drawback was the heat on stage. Fans had been drafted in but it was still stifling hot and our suits were beginning to smell pretty bad. I asked the manager if there was somewhere open on a Sunday where we could have them dry cleaned.

"Why do you guys insist on wearing those stupid suits all the time?" He asked.

"Well, it's part of the stage presentation." I answered.

"Listen," he said "you're in South Africa now, take this blank cheque, go and buy some white jeans and some white t-shirts, that will be dress enough and you won't be sweating your balls off."

The following Monday night, dressed all in white, we were amazed how much cooler and comfortable we were.

As I said, Sundays were our day off and South Africans would organise barbecues or "bries" as they called them, on those days. The weather was always so good that you could plan these outdoor events with little or no chance of bad weather interrupting them.

It only took a week or so for us to be invited by the locals to attend these gatherings. Everyone who came along to our shows was dressed casually in jeans, no t-shirts, so it was hard to tell how well off they were, or what their jobs were.

An example of this happened on my second Sunday off. Gordon and I had been talking to a Scots guy who had been in the country for a few years, and he had asked us to come to his house on that Sunday.

"Plenty wine, beer, food, and women," he said. "I'll get someone to pick you guys up." Sunday morning came and the phone rang in my room at eight-thirty. (They always started those damn bries too bloody early for me!)

"Brick" the receptionist said, "your transport is outside." I mumbled something about grabbing a quick shower. Washed and dressed, I pulled back the curtains and looked out onto the car park. It was empty apart from a grey Rolls Royce parked near the entrance. I phoned reception back.

"I haven't been that long, has he gone?"

"No, he's still there," she said.

"But there's only a Rolls Royce in the car park!" I told her.

"I know, it's for you two wasters, and just wait till you see the driver!" She said. I met Gordon in the hallway and headed to the car. There, waiting by the car holding the rear door open for us, was the driver, dressed in immaculate grey livery. I felt the sudden urge to wave like the queen as we pulled away, with the hotel staff gawping at us.

Apparently our host, whose name was Andy, was one of the top accountants in the country. The day was spent in the lap of luxury in a house an Arab sheik would be proud of, with every whim catered for. There were gorgeous girls everywhere, with perfect tanned bodies in tiny bikinis. At the beginning of the day, Andy had appeared with four crates of beer and thrown them into the huge pool by his main lounge door. I wondered if something had upset him and asked if he was ok.

"Sure, why shouldn't it be?" He asked. I mentioned the incident with the beer. "No, no," he laughed, "the fridges are full to bursting, so I throw the rest in the pool to keep cold, so if you want one, just dive in and help yourselves."

Andy had been a perfect host, and had given us a great day, and although he was well off, he was such a down to earth bloke, he endeared me to him and we became firm friends during my time there.

The next few weeks at "Samantha's" were very busy, with full houses every night. An added perk came our way. Local business men realising how popular we were started to sponsor us.

We would wear t-shirts with their company logo on them and we would receive favours in return. These favours resulted in us dining in the top restaurants, having haircuts, and designer clothing, all for free. The best of all was a B.M.W. open-top sports model which was put at our disposal for the duration of our stay there. Indeed, life was good.

No matter how good, there is always a down side, and although we were having the best experiences of a new and exciting lifestyle, there was the fact remaining that our friends and family were thousands of miles away. This brought on bouts of homesickness amongst us. "Samantha's" was doing so well that we had our contract extended to the full thirteen-week season there.

The phone call to my wife telling her of this development did not go down well. The other downside was that South Africa could be a very violent place. This was brought sharply home to us after a few weeks, when an incident involving Gordon occurred. We had finished our gig for the night and had gone our separate ways. Gordon had decided to stay and have a drink at the bar. As he was talking to some of the staff a pretty girl came up to him and bluntly told him, that if he put the Elvis suit on that he used in the act, he could take her to bed.

Gordon, not one to pass up a golden chance, told her his room number. This incensed the lady, who promptly turned on her heels, went
back to her table and informed her husband what Gordon had said!

Apparently, in the Cape area, to give your room number to a lady was treating her like a prostitute. (So we were told.) The fact that she had omitted to tell her hubby of her offer to Gordon did our lad no favours whatsoever.

"Who's in room two-one-nine!" Bellowed the furious spouse.

"I am," answered Gordon, turning to see

a mountain of a man charging toward him. Gordon, seeing the danger approaching, picked up the heavy bar stool he had been sitting on and threw it at him, only to see it bounce harmlessly off his chest.

The next thing he remembered was waking up in hospital, waiting for x-rays on his chest. Even though he was in agony, he had to give details of his bank account to pay for the said x-rays or nothing would be done. The deal completed, the x-rays were taken and revealed four cracked ribs. As he left, he was given the x-ray prints to take with him as he had paid for them. (Very thoughtful.)

Another incident was told to me by one of the regulars to the club. He and a friend had gone for a drive down the coast. They had stopped off for a beer in a small town and found a quiet little bar. The normal type of bar in that region was usually pretty basic, but this one was decked out in red carpets and drapes. The only thing that spoiled it was a gaping hole in the ceiling just over the bar area. The barman noticed the two men staring up at the ceiling.

"I see you're admiring the décor man," he said in a thick South African accent. "Well, I'll tell you how it happened," not waiting for a reply. "I'm working here two days ago and this kaffer (a derogatory term for a black man) walks in and as this being a multi-racial bar, I have to serve him." He leaned over to the men. "He was drunk, so I say, I'm not serving you man, you're too drunk. He demands a drink, so I say again, I won't serve you man, you are drunk! Three times I tell him to go away, but he just stands there giving me shit and pissing me off, so I pull out my gun and give him one in the chest."

With that, the barman reached below the counter and produced a double-barrelled shotgun. This alarmed our two reluctant listeners, especially the way the tale was being told.

"Did you hurt him much?" One of them asked.

"Hurt him! hurt him!, ha ha, I hurt him fucking dead, that's what I did!"

The two travellers exchanged frightened looks at each other, realising they were in the company of a murdering maniac.

"I can only thank god the carpet was red, didn't show the blood up too much!" He continued.

"What happened after that?" They asked, humouring the man while all the time keeping a wary eye on the firearm lying on the counter.

"Well, I phoned the cops of course," the barman said indignantly, "and I tells them I've got a dead kaffer in my bar who was drunk and pissed me off, so I had to shoot him. They turn up, drag the body out, ask to see the gun, then one of them asks for a couple of cartridges, loads the gun, and fires two shots into that ceiling."

By this time the barman was in hysterics as he related his tale. "You know what he says next?" He said, howling with laughter, "two warning shots, it was self-defence, imagine that! Self-defence eh!"

The two guys nervously laughed along with the man and took their leave as quickly as they could.

Chapter Seventeen
Johannesburg

Near the end of our contract at "Samantha's" we were paid a visit by the entertainments manager of one of the biggest Holiday Inns in the country. He liked what he saw and offered our agent another thirteen-week run in his cabaret lounge.

This made good business sense for everyone as the steady money would keep coming in for us and the agent. Added to the fact that the two hotels could now share the cost of our flights and expenses. This unfortunately did not go down to well with my wife, and relations became even more strained.

Our last night in "Samantha's" was highlighted after the show with a farewell party, which went on well into the early hours. The next morning, severely hung over, we packed our gear and were driven to the airport. We were astonished to see all the friends we had made in our short time waiting for us at the departure lounge. An impromptu party was held there and then with many bottles of champagne popped.

(A few being sprayed over us). This did not impress the airport staff who had to clean up the mess, or the airline who had to delay the flight by fifteen minutes because of the lengthy tearful goodbyes said by all.

Eventually five very drunk and champagne saturated Scotsmen managed to take their seats, oblivious to the hostile stares from their fellow passengers.

Johannesburg was a big sprawling city with multi-storey buildings and busy crowded streets, totally different from Cape Town. The President Hotel Holiday Inn was situated on the corner of Eloff and Plein Street in the town centre.

From the onset I didn't like the area and our accommodation were rooms on the fifteenth floor, based on two people sharing a room. Charlie and I decided to team up in one of the rooms. The cabaret room was called "The Jolly Roger" and was much bigger than "Samantha's" but very basic, with wooden floors, tables, and chairs.

Immediately I didn't take to the entertainments manager. He'd had a minor hit in the country in the seventies and regarded himself an authority on everything to do with showbusiness. His ideas on how we would be working were not what he had seen in Cape Town, and not what he had agreed to in the contract.

Whereas before, we were given free range on what was done on the shows, he now, in no uncertain terms told us he would be supervising everything. This became clear as the schedule was given to us for the coming weeks.

On Wednesday nights there was going to be mud wrestling. We were told we would be playing until eight-o-clock and then a team of scantily clad girls would take over the stage and fight each other in a giant mud pit. He cheerfully told us that we would be taking turns at refereeing these bouts in amongst the girls.

His next bombshell was that on certain nights, there would be strippers on and we would be the musical backing for them. When I complained bitterly about these tacky extra duties and that they were not in the contract, I was told in no uncertain terms again that this was how things were going to be done around here, as he was the boss, and I would do as I was told.

What made it worse was that the rest of the band, fearing a cancellation of the contract, had given in meekly to his demands. I asked to speak to him in private and had an unholy row with him stating that it had taken me eleven years to reach a high standard of professionalism, only for him to destroy it in less than a day. This did nothing to change his mind and the only thing gained by my outburst was that I was excused any of those embarrassing duties.

He had arranged a private show for the local press and business men a day before our three-month run was to begin. Food was laid on and a free bar was at their disposal. The show went well, with a standing ovation at the end.

However, as soon as the show was ended, the food was whisked away and the shutters came down in the bar area. This did not go down well with the media audience as they were used to being fawned over for favourable comments in their respective tabloids.

The inevitable happened the next morning when the first of the "write-ups" appeared in the press.

"What do they impersonate... a band?" Was the headline that screamed at us from the entertainment page. This was followed by two full columns describing us as the worst show to hit Johannesburg in twenty years. The rest of the local papers tried to outdo the first report in their assessments of the show in the days that followed and it was almost a week later before the critical bombardment came to an end.

An emergency meeting was called by the hotel top brass to find a solution to the crisis. The entertainments manager blamed us for a poor show (of course!) and we blamed him for being a cheapskate and upsetting the press and a stalemate ensued.

What nobody had noticed was that all the seats for the first evening's show had sold out. It appeared that the bad publicity had had the adverse effect on the public who had turned out in their droves to see this awful "pommy" band and were pleasantly surprised at the end of the show to find they were really pretty good. It didn't take long for the word to go round and after a few days, we had them queuing up to see us.

As the weeks went by, I was becoming more and more homesick. Big cities are not my favourite and my time at the President Hotel was one of the unhappiest of my life. The violence in Johannesburg was so apparent that white people were advised to stay out of the city centre from Saturday noon until Monday morning, unless in a crowd and even then, there were no guarantees of safety.

The majority of the local white population did not take to us "Aliens" either. An example of this happened as I was having a quiet drink on my own at a bar one night.

"Why don't you fuck off home, you pommy bastard!" Said a drunk, after hearing my accent. I politely told the slob that I was Scottish, and not from England.

"Well, fuck off home you Scottish pommy bastard!"

Charlie had gotten himself a girlfriend and had moved her into our room, which made me more miserable as there was nowhere I could find any privacy. I would wander aimlessly around the hotel on most days waiting for them to get out of bed before returning to the room.

At night they would have noisy lovemaking sessions, even though my bed was only a few feet away from them. My complaints to Charlie fell on deaf ears and I grew more and more depressed, wishing away the days until this nightmare contract was up and I could go home.

On the eleventh week our agent told us that he had secured another contract with a hotel on the other side of the city. Another thirteen weeks! Oh god! I was so down as I phoned home, waiting for another blazing row, but my wife seemed offhand and indifferent to the news. I reckoned she was as pissed off as I was and left it at that.

The "Mill Park" Holiday Inn was much smaller than the "President," as we found out on a spy trip a week before we started. The boss there welcomed us and told us we could do our own thing as long as we pulled the crowds in.

The "Pig and Whistle" music lounge was half the size of the "Jolly Roger," but much nicer, with an intimate feel about it. We all had a good feeling about it. The best news was being told that we had a house to live in instead of hotel accommodation. It was a large house with individual rooms for each of us. After six months of hotel living, with next to no privacy, this was like all my Christmas's coming at once.

The final night of the "Jolly Roger" arrived and skipping the party, with only a parting "fuck you" to the entertainments manager, I went upstairs to pack my case, ready to leave that God-awful place in the morning.

The house was about a mile from the hotel, and they had given us our own maid, Victoria, to keep the place tidy. (Some hope!) There was no washing machine so she did everything in the bath. I was always amazed how she managed to get everything spotless and ironed in this primitive way, considering she would wash our stage gear every evening after the show and they would be ready to wear, crisp and fresh the next evening.

As the weeks went by our stay at the "Jolly Roger" seemed like a bad dream. The crowds were good, the management were true to their word and let us do our own thing which led to a happy and profitable working environment on both sides. Christmas was approaching and I was missing my boys Paul and Bryan more and more.

It seemed I had been away from home for years. The only light at the end of the tunnel was the news that we had a definite date when we could go home at the end of January. I bought a calendar and ticked off the days as they passed. That Christmas of nineteen eighty-two was the worst I ever had. All the other guys had left the house to be with the girls they had gotten to know. I was the only one who hadn't fallen in love, keeping myself to casual relationships.

With extremely bad timing, I found myself in between one of these relationships on this Christmas Day, and after a few fruitless attempts at phoning home, I returned to an empty house to sit alone and drink myself into oblivion.

This may have had a bearing on the incident that happened a few days later. The Holiday Inns in the country had a deal with the South African forces which allowed their personnel to visit the hotels for free while on leave. Their army in particular had it very rough as they would be stationed on the border, fighting off communist backed guerrilla fighters.

After a month or so of living rough, and in constant danger, to be transported back to comfy beds and good food, in pleasant surroundings came as something of a shock to their systems. Most of the guys handled it pretty well, but there were always the few who were out to cause havoc and mayhem as a way of letting off steam.

One such group visited the "Pig" and immediately took a dislike to the band, and me in particular. Their barrage of abuse, directed mainly at me, lasted the whole evening and completely spoiled the show. The manager could see how upset we were and told us not to worry, as they had had their fun, and wouldn't be back.

The next night they were back again, even more offensive and noisier than before. The following two nights saw them sitting in the same seats, dishing out their foul treatment, once again, mainly at me. Clearly this situation couldn't continue, and I took matters into my own hands by talking to them at the break, trying to reason with them. I tried to explain to them how much they were spoiling it for the rest of the audience, who had paid good money. I was promptly told to "fuck off."

That night's pattern followed the same format as the previous evenings. All this personal abuse was getting me down and I turned up the next night with a feeling of dread, waiting for more of the same. To my surprise their usual table was occupied by different customers, and there was no sign of the troublesome morons anywhere.

We did the first part of the show in blissful comfort. I was relaxed and happier than I had been for many a day and was just getting ready to go on for the second half of the show, when the door burst open and in they came, drunken and louder than ever.

"Thought we weren't coming pommy, didn't you?" Yelled the ringleader, smirking at me. Something inside me snapped, and all the homesickness and loneliness exploded inside me in a silent rage. My professionalism went out the window.

"If you don't fuck off now, I'm gonna kick ten shades of shit out of you!" I screamed.

"Ooh, it looks like our little pommy friend has got some balls after all!" Laughed their leader.

"Come on then, let's take it outside." I'm not, and never have been a violent man, but at that moment, looking at his sneering face, all my pent-up emotions rose to the surface. I found myself following him to the door. As I stood outside listening to him goading me and telling the crowd which had gathered what he was going to do to me, a white fury came over me and I smacked him full force in the face. His nose disintegrated and he fell to the floor, where he promptly pissed his pants.

"Next!" I yelled at the stunned crowd. I waited, breathing heavily and ready for action, but as there were no takers, I turned on my heel and walked back into the room.

The next morning I was summoned to the managers office to be given a stern lecture about my behaviour on the previous evening.

"Jesus Christ man." he stormed. "We've got doormen to deal with that sort of trouble, do you realise that guy was a soldier, and therefore government property, you could go to jail for what you did last night!"

This made me regret my stupid action and wish even more I was back home in Scotland. The next two hours were spent in the office, with the manager making numerous phone calls to head office to sort out the mess.

Finally, he wearily replaced the telephone on its cradle and let out a deep sigh.

"Well, its fixed," he said. "No charges are being brought against you as there were witnesses to say you had been threatened, now get out of my office and no more trouble from you, or you are out on your ear!" Filled with relief, I thanked him and left.

The days went by and I ticked them off, one by one on my calendar until our final day in South Africa had arrived. Although we'd had the experience of a lifetime, living a lifestyle so very alien to our British way, we were bursting with excitement at the thought that within forty hours we would be back home.

Not everyone in the band was feeling the same. Charlie had fallen deeply in love with his girlfriend and Freddie had been smitten too, with a girl from Cape Town. The problems this would cause when we got home we're the last thing on my mind as I knew I would have a few of my own. The usual farewell party provided by the hotel was a rather sedate affair compared to the others as we were to be up very early to catch our flight.

Early or not, a dozen or so hardy souls were there to see us off at the airport. As our flight rose in the early morning sunny South African sky, I took a last look over the sprawling city of Johannesburg, reminiscing over the events of the past months, and happily settled down for the flight home.

Chapter Eighteen
The Berlin Wall

The journey home was a much more pleasurable experience as we were booked on a flight to London Gatwick airport. From there it was a quick change to Edinburgh. The total time taken on the return journey was fourteen hours compared to the twenty hours or so on the outward trip. (Must have made good money for the agent.)

We had gotten so used to the fine weather that it was a shock to our system when we stepped off the plane at Gatwick to be met by an icy February wind.

On arrival in Edinburgh we were met by an even icier wind and I was met by a slightly less icier reception from my wife. (Although not by much.) The kids gave me an uncomfortable hug as if they were greeting a stranger (which I suppose they were), but with the resilience of youth, within minutes they were begging to see what I'd brought them and I was "daddy "again.

As I walked to the car in the cold grey light of a Scottish morning it felt good to be home.

The trip to Africa was soon to leave us with casualties. Freddie had split from his wife and within a fortnight had his girl from Cape Town flown over to join him. This should have helped the band to function better, as he had been moping around like a love-sick bull and it was seriously affecting his performance. After only a short period it was apparent she was not going to settle in this cold climate of ours and Freddie dropped the bombshell that he was returning with her to Africa.

At the same time Charlie told us he was doing the same. Once again, the band was on the verge of folding. But Lady Luck once again came to our rescue. Gordon knew a drummer called Ian, from one of his previous bands. A quick phone call and a meeting was set up. Ian lived in Yorkshire, almost two hundred miles from the rest of us, but it would be no problem as he could stay with his sister in Edinburgh when we played locally.

As for replacing Charlie, it hadn't taken long for the news that we needed a guitarist to circulate around the cabaret scene and Alan appeared on our doorstep for an audition. He had long admired our show and had started his own comedy trio. His impressions were good enough and with the added bonus of the guitar playing, he was signed up. Once again, with a lot of rehearsals with our new members, we were ready for the road.

We also had to find a new roadie and as luck would have it, my nephew had just left school and was available. Roddie, or "Beaker" as he was nicknamed, was both a godsend and a devil's curse at the same time. He worked like a Trojan, but was always doing crazy things to wind me up and drive me to despair. After a few weeks working in Scotland we had another tour of Germany organised, but this time we were to include Berlin in the schedule.

The "Cold War "as it was called had been going on between Russia and the western powers for many years, with Berlin situated well inside the Russian territory which they captured from the Germans in the Second World War. Berlin itself had been divided into sectors between the British, American, French, and the Russians. To reach these sectors the Russians allowed the western powers a single road for access after passing through their various checkpoints. This was called the Berlin corridor.

We had been in Germany for a week, playing the garrison towns of Minden, Osnabruck, Bielefeld, etc and had been given accommodation in a small base near the first checkpoint to the corridor. I found out later that it was a listening and watching post to keep an eye on our Russian neighbours in the uneasy peace at the time.

The following morning before we set off, we were given an induction course by an American officer who was there to tell us what and what not to do passing through the corridor. A smartly dressed instructor greeted us as we took our seats facing a large screen in front of us.

"Good morning gentlemen," he drawled,

"can I ask who will be driving today?" (Me again.)

He pointed at me and said "this instruction mainly concerns you, but you other guys might want to listen up."

With that, he pulled down from the top of the screen a full-sized colour photograph of a soldier in a muddy brown uniform. "This is an East German soldier, you will know by the grey tabs on his collar."

Even though I was only three feet away from the screen, I had to look really intently to see the tabs he was talking about.

"The East German army has been initiated by the Russians and we do not recognise them as having any authority over our forces, therefore, they have no right to stop you on your journey. If one of these guys stands in the road in front of you, you will not stop, and will continue your journey as planned."

He went back to the screen and pulled down another full sized photograph of another soldier in an identical muddy brown uniform.

"This is a Russian soldier," he said, "You will recognise him by the red tabs on his collar."

Once again, I had to look carefully at the screen to see the markings around his neck.

"If this guy stands in front of you, you will stop and display this sign on the windscreen, which will tell him in Russian that you wish for a competent English speaking officer to be present to inform you as to why you have been interrupted on your journey through the corridor."

With that, he came over and handed me a plastic Union Jack flag with Russian writing on it.

"You will follow the yellow signs and only the yellow signs throughout your journey, and please do not get lost or leave the route designated, as you will be in Russian territory, which could cause a lot of shit hitting the fan getting you back. Finally," he said, "the corridor is a set distance between the checkpoints you will be travelling through, so you are required to drive at forty miles per hour, no more, no less. It is estimated that your journey will take two and a half hours to complete, if you arrive in two hours, you will incur a speeding fine, if you haven't arrived by the time three hours have elapsed, the Russians will come looking for you with the assumption that you are spying."

He paused for a moment to let the facts sink in. "Gentlemen, have we any questions?" He asked.

My hand shot up. I told him of my concerns over the fact that, with me travelling at forty miles an hour, and a guy in a muddy brown uniform suddenly jumping out in front of me, by the time I had identified the colour on his lapel, he would be a flattened bloody mess in the road.

The instructor looked at me coldly and said, "Use your discretion." (that is what I call a cop-out!)

An hour later, with me hoping not to have to "use my discretion," we set off.

The first stop after leaving the Western sector was the East German checkpoint. Although they had no authority, they could if they wished, hold you up at their barrier for as long as they pleased. We were told it would be advisable to sit quietly in the van and wait and give them no reason to hold us up any longer than necessary.

It was quite eerie sitting there with no one in sight and only their watchtower with its one way glass fitted to let them see us, but we couldn't see them.

After about fifteen minutes the automatic barrier lifted suddenly, and we passed through onto the Russian checkpoint a short distance farther on. This was a completely different kettle of fish. The personnel at the base had told us exactly what to do and how to behave.

The procedure was as follows. One person would have his name on the document required for stamping for entry into the corridor. This person would be the only person allowed to leave the vehicle at the checkpoint. All other persons must remain inside the vehicle at all times. Any unauthorised persons attempting to leave the vehicle would be liable to arrest, or worse, shot. The allocated person, with paper in hand, would leave the vehicle, march smartly up to the waiting sentry on duty, give a regulation salute, and hand him the document.

The sentry would return his salute; inspect the paper leaving the allocated person by the sentry box. The sentry would then approach the vehicle and check the registration plates and the number of occupants, etc. Having satisfied himself that all was in order, he would return to his box, salute the person again, receive a salute in return, and hand back the paper.

The allocated person would then take the paper into the office to be inspected again before being stamped. Having had the paperwork passed the person would return to the sentry, hand over the paper again whilst saluting again.

The guard would inspect the document after returning his salute, return said paper to said person, salute again and receive a salute in return. Said person would return to the vehicle, the barrier would be lifted and we would be on our way.

All very straightforward, if a bit over the top you might think. Unfortunately, not for us. We, in our misguided wisdom, had decided that "Beaker," being only sixteen, should take the paper as it would be an experience to tell all his mates back home how he had met the Russians.

I say unfortunately, because at the base the night before, he'd had a lot to drink (an understatement) and was still as drunk as a skunk as we approached the Russian checkpoint.

As the van pulled up to a stop at the barrier, Beaker slid the van door open and promptly fell flat on his face in a large puddle in the road. The Russian guard, immaculate in his uniform, stood ramrod straight by his sentry box, with only his eyes following Beaker with loathing.

Giggling like a schoolgirl, Beaker staggered to his feet and tried to dry himself off, using the transit paper in his hand. Everyone was screaming at him from the van, but this went unnoticed by the drunken idiot.

"Don't worry, got it all under control," he slurred, tapping his nose in a knowledgeable way. He lurched over to the guard. "Here pal," he said, waving the sodden document in his face. The Russian stiffened even more and gave our swaying friend a copybook Russian salute straight from the regulation manual.

"Here!" Said Beaker, in annoyance. "Take the fucking thing, I ain't got all day!" As he tried to shove the paper into the guard's hand. The Russian repeated his immaculate salute, staring rigidly straight ahead.

"What's wrong with this prick?" Complained Beaker, turning to us in exasperation.

"You're supposed to salute him!" I roared.

"Oh yeah!" he said, realising his mistake. Facing the guard, he gave him a salute that could only be likened to someone having a quick scratch of his forehead. This did not impress the guard one little bit as he began to salute continuously, still staring straight ahead of him, and probably wishing Beaker would just disappear.

"Salute him or I'm going to fucking kill you!" I bellowed. By this time our lad was in fits of laughter, regarding the whole escapade as a big joke.

"Has someone wound this twat up at the back?" he said.

"Salute him!" We all screamed at the same time.

"All right, all right, no need to get your knickers in a twist!" Slurred our drunken representative. He turned to face the guard and gave a near perfect British salute. This finally passed inspection with the guard who immediately stopped saluting and took the wet paper from his hand.

As he approached the van, Beaker decided to follow him.

"You're supposed to stay by the sentry box!" I yelled.

"Jesus Christ, there's too much fucking about with this job!" He complained, and grudgingly returned to the box. Having finished his inspection, the soldier returned to his box to find that Beaker had gone inside it. This did not go down well with him and he began yelling something in Russian, while forcibly ejecting our lad out of his box.

Once out in the open again, a very angry guard saluted Beaker once more and handed him back the paper. This time our alcoholic idiot presented a perfect salute in return and received the document without a hitch. The rest of the procedure went as planned and it was with much relief when at last, we saw the barrier being lifted and were ushered in our way.

"You really pissed that guy off you arsehole!" I said.

"He'll be even more pissed off when he sees I've puked up in his sentry box!" Said Beaker with a smirk.

The journey through the corridor passed without incident and after passing through the various checkpoints at the other side, we eventually entered West Berlin. It was, as I said earlier, a city divided. The west was a vibrant bustling metropolis, whereas the east side was dull and grey as if left in a time warp from the war.

The Russians had built a wall between the the two sides of the city in the sixties, dividing friends and family. Looking at this monument to inhumanity, it was hard to realise that a few feet of concrete could separate and affect so many people. All along the wall on the western side was graffiti decrying the segregation and in certain places a cross would mark the spot where some poor soul had been killed trying to escape from the eastern sector. It shocked and saddened me, and also scared me to think what our Russian "allies" were capable of.

We had two gigs in the city. The first being at the R.A.F. base there. It was an R.A.F. base in name only as the Russians would only allow supply planes to land there and no warplanes were to be stationed on it. The gig went well and we were given accommodation in the sergeant's mess.

I woke up abruptly at about six o'clock the next morning, with my room shaking and a thunderous noise blasting in my eardrums. I thought "Christ, an earthquake in Berlin!" I ran downstairs and found the duty orderly sitting casually at his desk. "What's happening?" I asked, in a panic.

"You mean that fucking racket out there?" He asked, picking his teeth with a pen.

"Well," he continued, "you see where the wall is over there?" He indicated to the dreaded barrier, which was only about twenty feet from the mess. "Behind that wall are about fifty Russian tanks warming up their engines."

I asked why. "They do that every morning just to let us know that they are there, and they could come through that wall at any time, cos we've fuck all to stop em with!"

I said that surely we must have some defence.

"Yeah, I've got my defence," he said, "it's a motorbike in the shed outside and I'll be on it!"

The second gig did not go so well. There were two regiments based at the barracks we were playing. One was the Gloucesters and the other was the Kings Own Scottish Borderers. An English and a Scottish regiment, not a good mix. In civilian life there would have been a lot of national pride and rivalry, but in the forces it was much more intense than that.

Some idiot in charge had decided that to save money he would put the show on for one night instead of two and get the two regiments to share. Before the show began long rows of chairs had been set out in the room, but as we started there was suddenly a five-foot gap running right down the middle of the hall. This became the "no-man's land" of the pitched battle that followed.

We struggled to keep the show going, but as the two regiments were more intent on tearing each other to pieces it was impossible for us to carry on and, still in our stage suits, we dragged our equipment out through the rear doors to safety.

We had two days free to enjoy the sights of West Berlin before continuing our tour. As I had said, it was a vibrant city where everyone lived for the day, as the constant threat of a

Russian invasion was never far from their minds. We saw the flame of peace, which had burned continuously for many years, (until a bunch of drunken soldiers had put it out by pissing on it!)

There was Spandau prison which had only one inmate. That was Rudolph Hess, who had been Hitler's henchman during the war. It was strange to pass the prison at night and see the one solitary light from his cell in an otherwise darkened building. We enjoyed the atmosphere of the busy bars and discos, but all the time the dark and dreary existence beyond that cursed wall was never far from our minds.

Chapter Nineteen
On the Telly

Eddie had some great news on our return to Scotland.

"I've got you an audition for a TV show!" He said. "It's that one with the dusty bin in it." The show was a quiz show called 3-2-1 and was one of the most popular on television at that time, with a prime-time viewing spot on a Saturday evening.

Although it was a quiz show, it was interlaced with cabaret acts. Our audition was scheduled for four days after our return and we had to work out a three-minute spot. After a great deal of rehearsals, spending most of the days trying this format and that, we had our condensed act ready. The hard work paid off as the producers were pleased with what they saw and signed us up for the show.

The show was being recorded four weeks later and we spent time telling anyone who would listen about our big break. My dear old mum was in her element, telling everybody, from her cronies at the bingo hall, to the girls in the knitting club that her boy was going to be on the telly.

The news also led to a lot of interest from the local press, which got us a few write-ups and free publicity. Surprisingly, the fee we were being paid for the show was not that good, but the expenses we incurred must have gotten into four figures!

The show's producers had decided that our stage suits were not "camera friendly" and wanted us kitted out in new attire. This meant a trip to London to have suits made by the top theatrical tailors based on the Kings road. The day of the fitting fell on the middle of a busy period of club shows for us. That day saw us catch a very early train from Edinburgh to the capital, have our fitting and returning immediately to Edinburgh to do an evening show. As the trip took over thirteen hours there and back, it was a very jaded performance that night.

The show was being televised by Yorkshire Television and there were to be five other acts on the show besides us. The other acts were given accommodation in the best hotel in Leeds and although we were offered the same, Ian had in-laws in the area and we were going to stay with them.

This worked out really well for us as we pocketed the cash intended for the hotel. (Ah, we canny Scots!) It led to a surreal situation where we were performing on national television, and the previous evening, had been wrapped up in our sleeping bags on the in-laws living room floor!

The show's host was a guy called Ted Rogers. He was a lovely chap who made us all feel welcome and helped to settle our nerves a bit. Ian had somehow got his hands on some tickets for his family. Ted always made his entrance by walking down the aisle steps in the centre of the seated audience stopping to shake a hand here and there. Ian had got seats right next to the aisle he would be coming down. He cheekily asked Ted if he would stop and shake his father-in-law's hand as he passed by.

Ted, god bless him, not only agreed, but rehearsed his hand shaking manoeuvre at the designated seat a few times to make sure there were no slip-ups. Unfortunately, on the night, he got his bearings completely wrong and missed Ian's father-in-law by two rows. The result was a startled man having his hand shaked vigorously as though he was an old friend of Ted's and being called by a completely different name to his own.

As we were to be the last act on, we had to wait around until the rest of them had done their stints and the producers were happy with the footage on film. This meant that one or two of the acts had numerous "takes" to get it right and resulted in the time allocated to the show drawing ever closer to the finish.

Finally, after what seemed like an age, it was our turn. It was then a bombshell was dropped on us. Because of all the delays and re-runs we would only get one "take." If it wasn't satisfactory, we would not be included in the show! It looked as though our chance for fame and stardom was being snatched from us. The pressure on every one of us was immense. This wasn't helped by a stagehand who cockily told us that, if we made it onto the show, there would probably be about twelve million people watching on the night it was to be screened.

Finally, our moment had arrived and we went through our act. I don't remember much of it as I was too busy concentrating on getting my cue's right, but at the end I felt it must have been okay as the audience burst into loud applause.

After the show, in the hospitality room, we kept asking the people in charge if we had done alright and were told that everything was fine and not to worry.

We were back in Germany when the show was eventually televised, doing the usual round of army camps. We were very apprehensive, as we had no idea how we would come across on the screen as we hadn't even seen the replay of it.

To put me out of my misery, I phoned my dad when the show would have finished to see how it had gone.

"Aye, it was alright," he said casually.

"What, just alright?" I said. I could hear the phone being jostled violently and my mum's voice broke in.

"Ooh son! you were brilliant, I can't wait to see the girls down at the club and auntie

Agnes thought you were all great too! You were just like TV stars!" (More phone jostling.)

"Are you there son?"(Dad again.) "Was that make-up you were wearing?"

I explained that we had to wear it for the cameras.

"So, you are not gay then?"

"No dad," I sighed wearily, "It's just for the cameras."

"That's alright then!" He said and promptly put the phone down.

Our first inkling of how well we had done on the show was when we arrived back in England. We pulled into a service station soon after disembarking from the ferry. Having fuelled up, we went inside to get some snacks for the journey. As we waited in the queue I noticed some of the people there staring at us. One of them plucked up the courage and blurted out. "Hey, aren't you that lot on the telly, you know, three, two, one?"

We said we were, and before we knew it we were signing autographs to all and sundry. With all the commotion and congratulations and the cheery waves goodbye no one, (including ourselves) had noticed we hadn't paid for the fuel or snacks. It was beginning to look like we had found that elusive fame at last.

Chapter Twenty
The Emerald Isle

The exposure on television had certainly done the trick. Wherever we went, the signs on the posters for our show had, "stars of 3,2,1" plastered all over them. We were committed to the shows that had been contracted before the telly appearance, so nothing had radically changed. (Nor had the fee.)

After a few weeks of local gigs, Eddie called us into his office.

"I've got you a spot on the Late Late Show in Dublin." He said.

Seemingly this show was as big in Ireland as 3,2,1 was in the U.K. It was hosted by a guy called Gay Burns who was massively popular there.

"It'll work out well because I've got you three weeks gigs before the show in the Belfast area!" He said.

"Belfast!" We all yelled back as one. "Aren't they blowing a lot of things up there at the moment, like people?" Asked Alan sarcastically.

"Yes, but you will be doing shows mainly for the troops so you will be well looked after," he said. When I said he would probably enjoy a trip over there with us, it was immediately turned down as he had too much to do in the office. (Yeah, right).

This was the period in Ireland they casually called "the troubles". The problem had been caused by the country being divided up in the early part of the twentieth century. The Irish had risen up against British rule and to appease them, the government had given them home rule, but had kept a section in the North under their control. This area became known as Ulster, where it was mainly inhabited by members of the Protestant faith.

The Catholic South, or Eire as it was called, had regarded this as a thorn in their side and certain factions had decided that violence was the only way to make Britain bend to their ways and unite the country as one.

The Protestants in the North regarded themselves as British and waved a similar violent war against the South. This led to almost daily violence and explosions in the Ulster region, (mainly in Belfast.) The British army had been sent in to keep the peace and this had only incensed the catholic population and made them the prime target.

It was not a happy bunch of musicians who boarded the Stranraer to Larne ferry crossing the Irish Sea. It was made all the less happy knowing that a few years earlier, a local Irish band had been held up by one of the militant groups, dragged from their van and shot for doing exactly what we were about to do.

We knew all about the religious divide

between the catholic and protestant faiths as this was ever present, if not as violent in Scotland. With this knowledge Eddie had felt sure we could take care of any tricky situation that would present itself. (From the safety of his office in Scotland.)

The stark reality hit us on reaching our first army camp gig. Where, as in Germany you would have a sentry by a single pole barrier to check your credentials, here were sandbagged machine gun posts and heavy metal gates barring your way. High ridged speed bumps made it impossible to approach the gate at any more than a walking pace for your vehicle. No matter who you were, if you were not normally known to the garrison, guns would be trained on you while the guards pushed a large mirror on a trolley under your vehicle to check for bombs that might be attached there.

Our gig went well that night. The majority of the troops were younger than average and we expected the usual tough time, but as so few British acts came over because of the troubles; they warmly took to us and in a way regarded us as one of them. As we sat in a café on our way to the fifth gig the horror of the conflict hit home to us personally. Two off duty soldiers had somehow driven into the area where an I.R.A. funeral procession was taking place. They had been recognised as army personnel, hauled out of their car and beaten to death by the angry mob.

All this was televised on the news. Arriving at the gig we found out that we were at the poor guy's base. We immediately contacted the people in charge to cancel the show. The regimental sergeant major marched up to us.

"What's all this about cancelling the show, you'll do no such fucking thing!" He raged. "We will not let those bastards beat us down, do you understand me, the show goes on as planned." And on the show went.

They laughed at every joke and sketch, applauded the music and gave us a standing ovation at the end. The poignant moment came at the end when the R.S.M. took the microphone and raised a glass to their fallen comrades. To a man there was not a dry eye in the house.

A few more shows combining civilian and army gigs and we headed south to Dublin for our spot on the Late Late Show. The first noticeable thing about Dublin was how expensive everything was. Our fee for the show was above average, but we soon realised that this would barely cover our expenses.

Arriving at the studio it was worrying that no one had any clue who or what we were, or why we were there. As for the host Gay Byrne, he was never told about any of the guests until he read the script on the night. After a couple of phone calls between our agent and their producer, we had been given the go ahead.

In the end, the show did us no favours. As we were flung at them at the last minute they didn't know quite what to do with us. We were put on right at the start, with the audience barely sat in their seats. Our three and a half minutes were met with bemused silence and the only sounds of laughter found was coming from Beaker our roadie who was in fits of laughter at our discomfort.

Show done, we immediately set off back to Ulster to catch the early ferry from Larne. It was with a fair amount of relief, coming through the tour unscathed, that we watched the shores of the Emerald Isle fade into the distance.

Chapter Twenty-One
Deutschland Again

No sooner were we home than another NAAFI tour in Germany was on the cards. It was the summer ball season where the army dressed up in all their finery and no expense was spared on those special nights.

On this trip we had a comedian called Johnny Hammond with us he was of mature years and had been doing the north east circuit for a long time. He had us in stitches with his experiences. One I recall is when he turned up at a club in Sunderland. There were police cars with blue lights flashing all over the place.

"Christ!" He thought, "I haven't even been on yet!"

As he entered the club, he was stopped by a few of the committee. "Johnny glad you are here, we've got a bit of a problem." One of the committee members said. "There's a young lad in the front row, he's taken a brainstorm and shot his dad in the leg with the pistol his dad brought home from the war and as it's Sunday he has come down to the club for the usual strippers and comedians." They ushered Johnny to the stage curtain and peering through, sure enough, there was the lad in the front row, sitting there with the gun on the table.

The thing that amazed Johnny was that no one seemed to mind and just carried on as normal.

"There are some CID coppers in the audience, so what we want you to do is grab his attention so these guys can nick him."

Well Johnny thought about all this for a micro second. "You can fuck off!" Came the reply.

"But Johnny, the strippers going to go on."

Johnny had a think about it before responding. "Well I'm a professional and a man, and no woman is going to make me look like a coward, so I'll do it." He said.

Come the time for the show and the stripper managed to do her routine, racing across the stage and fully naked in fifteen seconds flat.

"Right Johnny, you're on," Said a committee man.

Johnny shuffled nervously to the centre of the stage and began his routine. After five minutes, the only person who was laughing was the young guy with a gun. As the plain clothed policemen grappled him to the ground and began hauling him away in handcuffs, Johnny shouted, "Leave him here and throw the rest of these miserable bastards out!"

Another instance he recalled was a story about a singer who was sent to a club in Hartlepool. (I can't remember the name.) I only played there once and had heard the story of the

Hartlepool monkey. Seemingly, during the Napoleonic wars, a French ship has run aground by its shores and although the crew had long abandoned it, they had left their pet monkey, dressed in a French navy uniform on board.

As the Hartlepudlians had never seen a French man before, they assumed the monkey was one. The monkey was put on trial and because it wouldn't defend itself was hung as a spy! When I asked a local if this was the town that hung a monkey, I was told "and there's plenty more rope for ye as well, lad."

They are still touchy about it.

Anyway I digress, back to the singer. The club he had been booked to play had a reputation of having a really-hard audience to please. As he walked on to the stage, the usual wall of noise of the chatty crowd greeted him. Still being totally ignored, he began to look around him in wonder, still not saying a word.

After a few minutes of this, the crowd began to take notice and quietened down considerably. Eventually a hushed and intrigued audience fell silent and stared at him in puzzlement. Picking the right moment, he boomed "Ladies and Gentlemen, what a privilege to be asked to come here tonight." He stamped his foot on the stage floor. "You see that," He said pointing to the floor, "that is not your plywood or chipboard that, it's teak!" (A few mutters of approval from the crowd.)

He sauntered over to the stage curtains, rubbing them between his fingers. "And these curtains, not nylon or the like for here... velvet!" (Loud mummering from the crowd.) "And that carpet that your chairs are sitting on, Axminster!" (Loud applause.) "It just shows how the common man, by the sweat of his brow, can drag himself from the depths of the earth and erect the monuments of excellence such as this!" (Deafening applause.) He paused for a moment. "And then they open the doors and let you arseholes in!" (Police escort from the premises.)

Our first night was in Minden, in an old S.S. barracks. The sergeant's mess was on the fourth floor up, which did not impress our Beaker one bit. With the reluctant help of four press ganged squaddies we managed to haul our six tons of gear up the old staircases. The sergeant in charge looked ruefully at all the equipment and decided that the power supply would not take the load.

"We'll get one of the generators from ordinance. That will give us the juice needed." He said.

With the generator in place and the supply cable winched up the outside of the building and through the open window to the stage, we tested it out in our sound check and all seemed well. Into the first two minutes of the show, the power failed and everything stopped.

The sergeant, wearing his best uniform, rushed up to see what was wrong.

"What's happened?" He asked in a panic.

"Powers gone!" I answered.

He grabbed a young squaddie on bar duty and sent him down to see what the problem was. He returned a few minutes later, gasping for breath after running up all those stairs, to say that the generator had tripped out.

"Well switch it back on then, you fucking arsehole!"

The sergeant, aware that the crowd were getting restless and that this show was his responsibility. Off went the poor squaddie and within a couple of minutes the power was back on.

Off we started again, and once again, within two minutes, the power cut out. The poor guy in charge was distraught as this was his night to shine in front of all his colleagues, and it was going down the pan quickly.

"Must be a faulty generator," he said, taking logical control of the situation. "You two, get over to ordinance and bring up another generator," he said, pointing to two lads who were supposed to be on table service.

Five minutes later saw a replacement generator in place and said cables connected. The show began again only to stop at almost the same time as the other two attempts.

"I don't understand it, one of these things

should be able to power a small village!" Said the sergeant, almost in tears as the crowd were growing more and more restless. As we puzzled what to do next, a soldier on duty at the guard room appeared and handed the poor sergeant a note.

It was from a captain who was housed near the sergeant's mess. He was complaining about the noise the generator was making and had twice ordered it to be shut down only to find that it had been started up again. The resilient sergeant quickly resolved the problem by inviting the captain as a special guest to the party, with free food and drink which he readily accepted (and made good use of.) The rest of the night passed off without a hitch and the sergeant' reputation was restored.

The tour continued well, but nothing ever runs smoothly forever and it was shown to be at the later stage of it. We were booked to play for the Royal Green Jackets and arrived to find a rather hostile reception towards us. Each camp we played was different from each other, but this one definitely did not seem to take to "civvies "in their midst.

Normally, we were treated well, with food and accommodation. Here, we were grudgingly told we could eat in the canteen, but as we sat down with our meal we noticed there was no cutlery on the table. When we asked for some we were told that you had to bring your own. We were so hungry, having travelled all day with no break, that we ate it with our hands, to the pleasure of the laughing squaddies watching us. The NAAFI manager then told us we would be given two drinks each and no more at the show. Normally there was no restriction on how much we drank.

Expecting the worst, we started the show. The barracking and abuse was so loud that we could barely hear ourselves. They kept this up for the whole show, but we stuck to our guns and finished the gig. More trouble was to come when a few of the squaddies decided they wanted to have a go with our guitars and drums. When we refused point blank the situation grew so ugly that the M.P.s had to be called in to clear the hall.

We sat in the quiet aftermath, physically and mentally drained. As we packed away the gear, the manager approached us.

"You did a good job to hold these bastards at bay, they like fuck all apart from causing trouble, I admire your spirit lads, come and have a drink, I think you all deserve it."

As the evening went on, the alcohol kept coming as he recounted his exploits of the time he was in the forces and we didn't notice how the time had flown until the duty sergeant appeared to tell us it was time to call a halt.

"Don't get your knickers in a twist," the manager said, "sit down and have a drink with us."

"I shouldn't really, being on duty, but I suppose one won't hurt," replied the sergeant.

A few hours later, and many more drinks drunk, we were trying to force-feed the poor guy with a jar of mussels as he sat slumped in a chair in a comatose state. We eventually bade our farewells, after many more toasts to the band, the manager, her majesty, the armed forces (apart from those Green Jacket bastards!) and an even more drunken duty sergeant, who by this time had slid to the floor, lying in a pool of mussels and vinegar.

The next day, on our way to the next gig we tuned into the forces network to hear that we were to be watched carefully when we came to any of the camps in the area as a NAAFI manager who was a reformed alcoholic had packed a suitcase with bottles of spirits and disappeared, while the duty sergeant had been found by the person who was to take over from him and promptly put on a charge for being drunk on duty.

Our last gig of the tour was in a little town called Lemgo and as luck would have it, we were housed in a small hotel outside the barracks. It was a lovely old-fashioned town with wooden buildings and cobbled streets, but the forces had managed to upset the locals as we found out when we went for a drink in the centre.

As we ordered our beers in a little bar, a stony-faced barman flipped a sign above our heads to face us. "No English served here." It said.

"We're no English, we're Scottish", I said smugly. The barman then flipped a sign saying "no Scottish served here," followed by "no Irish served here" and finally, "no Welsh served here." We got the hint and left.

The digs were much friendlier and we passed a pleasant hour or two chatting to the landlord and landlady at their bar. He was a big jolly chap while his wife was very shy and demure.

Above the bar was a glass case with about a dozen ends of neckties arranged like medals in it. Intrigued, I asked the host what the significance was.

"Ah, mein Herr, here we have an age-old traditional ceremony where the ladies on a certain day of the year, can dress up, wear a mask so as no one can recognise them and take to the streets. When they see a man who has a pleasing appearance to them, they cut off the bottom of their tie and take it for a trophy. In return the gentleman can take her home for the night to do as he pleases."

I looked at the ties in the trophy case.

"Yes, before you ask, these are my wife's." I looked down from the ties to this shy little woman and realised you can never judge a book by its cover.

Chapter Twenty-Two
Ellen Vannen

As the weeks and months went by, we began to realise that the television exposure had not brought the major breakthrough we had hoped for.

Although the venues had improved and we were on the main circuits, there were already one or two comedy bands already on the national television channels and therefore no need for another one. Even so, the television slot managed to secure our first summer season on the Isle of Man in nineteen eighty-five. It was an eleven-week run in a place called the Falcon Cliff just outside the main town of Douglas.

As we approached the island we could see all the brightly coloured hotels and guest houses lined along the promenade, with the Falcon Cliff like a White Castle, sitting high on the hill above to the side of the town. Our digs were in the Premier Hotel situated on the Queens promenade, and although we had to share two or three to a room at first, our hosts Dorothy and Ken made us more than welcome. (I returned many years later and the gaily coloured hotels were now a drab stone and sadly the Premier was no more.)

Having settled in and the gear up and checked in the venue, we readied ourselves for the opening night. This was a free night for the hoteliers and guest house owners to come and see what the act could do. If they liked what they saw, then by word of mouth and leaflets left for the guests, the season should be successful.

However, if we didn't impress, it was going to be a long, hard eleven weeks. Luckily everyone enjoyed the show and even though they had seen many shows before, gave us a great reception. This pleased our landlady Dorothy the most as it gave her the bragging rights to have the best show on the island staying with her. (Her own words.)

The complementary show had done its work as from the first week the hall was packed out, with people queuing all the way down the hill, waiting for a seat. Within a few days we had it down to a fine art at the finish of the show, where the audience would be on their feet clapping and shouting for another encore, while we would be off stage, changed and watching them from the fire escape steps before we headed to our hotel bar to celebrate.

This was a great time for us as we only had to play for an hour or so and then could party well into the night. The same could not be said for poor Ken, our landlord. He would be up most of the night with us serving drinks and then had to be up at the crack of dawn to start preparing breakfast for the guests.

The poor guy stuck it out for nearly a fortnight before finally admitting defeat.

"Look lads," he said wearily, "I can't keep this up any longer, I'm going to have to shut the bar at two o'clock in future."

Gordon and I thought for a moment and came up with the suggestion that we could run the late bar for him to let him have a rest. We assured him that there would be no fiddling going on and anyway, we were going to be there for some time and we would be found out sooner or later. He thought for a moment and warily agreed; stating that the money we spent of a night would be sadly missed if he closed early.

After a quick instruction on how to work the pumps and the till, Gordon and I worked out our rota and started the following night.

We soon got the hang of it and after a few days Ken grew to trust us and enjoyed his well-earned rest. The majority of the tourists coming to the island were from Ireland and on the whole were very nice people to know, but there are always exceptions.

My experience of this occurred at the end of my third stint behind the bar. A little guy had just booked in and had come straight downstairs for a drink.

"I'll have a double whiskey and put another one in it," he demanded.

"You mean a treble whiskey?" I corrected him.

"No ya eejit! I said a double and put

another in it, are ye not all there?" He shouted, pointing his finger at his temple.

I bit my tongue and poured a treble out for him.

"I'll be sitting over there." He said, pointing at the farthest table in the bar, "bring it over, and don't take as long as it took ye to pour it." Considering his drink was there right in front of him I thought this was extremely rude, but I dutifully placed it on a tray and took it to him.

This went on for most of the two weeks of his stay, with him always demanding and never a thank you or a courtesy of any kind in return. Nearing the end of his stay, which he had spent day and night in the bar, never venturing out other than to buy a newspaper, he asked about the entertainment on the island.

"Well, the best show is at the Falcon Cliff, a really good cabaret act."

"Get me a ticket for Friday," he demanded.

Got you, you ignorant bastard! I thought. When he sees me up there on stage he'll realise that he should never treat people like dirt as they might have hidden talents. I made sure he had a front row seat facing me so he could not help but notice the "star" that I was.

Friday night came and I had a little chuckle to myself as I imagined the look on his face when he saw me. The curtains opened and the lights went up and sure enough, the look on his startled face was a picture as he spotted me in my stage gear.

"Fuck me!" He screamed, jumping to his feet, "that's me fucking barman!" (Sigh, not the response I was hoping for.)

The Isle of Man is a beautiful place and although it is quite small, the scenery changes with almost every mile. It is steeped in folklore and tradition with its own government and money. I was sitting at the bar in the Falcon Cliff one day talking to a local.

"Do you know that there is a law on the island which has been in force for a thousand years, and has never been rescinded," he said. "It says that on a certain day of the year, a Manx man can kill a Scotsman and not be prosecuted." When I asked what day that was, he just gave me a wry smile and said, "I'm not telling you."

I loved my time on the island. The work was easy in comparison to the norm of loading and unloading gear and travelling hundreds of miles up and down motorways. The night life was great and it didn't take me long to make a new circle of friends. What made it all the better was that most of the band had moved to other digs so we only had to meet up for rehearsals or the gig and weren't in each other's faces all the time. As I mentioned previously, Bobby and I were not on the best of terms so this arrangement suited us both.

The weeks seemed to fly by and before long it was almost time to go home. But before we did, it was time for the famous motorcycle races to be held. The T.T. Race was held earlier in the year, with the Grand Prix in September. The locals assured me that the T.T. Event was far better than the Grand Prix but I still got caught up in the excitement of the occasion. The island was crammed to bursting with bikes and bikers from all over the world to watch the event.

Two of the race teams had booked into our hotel. One was a sponsored team with two bikes in different classes, with the rider, mechanics, manager, etc, while the other was a two-man team of rider and mechanic. Such was the atmosphere of friendship and common interest that there was no one-upmanship between the two teams and they all got along really well together.

Gordon and I got passes to the stand for the races. The first race included our sponsored team, who came a very credible fifth, so we went to the contestants' tents at the rear to celebrate with them. I have always had a soft spot for the underdog, so when the other team's race started, I went down to the pits with the mechanic to watch the riders' progress.

With the race half way through, things were going well for him as he was in the front pack of leaders, when a message came over the Tannoy asking the mechanic to report to the steward's office.

"This doesn't sound good" he said and rushed off to find out what the trouble was. He returned five minutes later with a look of sheer terror on his face.

"He's gonna kill me!" he said, "he's gonna fucking kill me!" he repeated.

I asked him to calm down and tell me what was wrong.

"A wheel has come off his bike, I mustn't have tightened it up properly, he's gonna kill me!"

"Is he all right?" I asked.

"Oh yeah, just skinned his arse and elbow, that's the trouble, it won't stop him tearing me apart!"

When I asked what would happen next, he told me he was supposed to pick him up but he was so frightened what would happen to him that he had got someone else to get him. He picked up his jacket and made a beeline for the exit.

Half an hour later, a very angry rider with torn and tattered leathers hanging from his backside and elbows limped into the pits.

"Where is he? Where is that useless bastard?" He yelled.

I told him he had gone.

"Just as well, cos at the moment I'd rip his balls off!" We went to the tent to join the other team and after a few drinks, he mellowed and even cracked some jokes about his mishap. (Strange breed these bikers.)

Back at the hotel there was no sign of the poor guy. We presumed he had hightailed it to the first available ferry home to escape the wrath of his rider. The next morning at breakfast he poked his head sheepishly round the door.

"Mate, I'm really sorry, it was a stupid mistake and I can't apologise enough." Without a word being spoken, the rider, and all the members of the other team rose from their tables, went out into the hallway, picked up the poor wretch and stretchered him across the road to the sea wall. With three great swings to gain momentum, they threw him over the wall and into the sea. Still without a word being spoken, they returned to finish their breakfast.

"Did anyone notice if the tide was in." I asked, fearing he might have broken his neck or something.

"Nope" came the riders casual reply, "but I hope not."

"Why?" I asked.

"Poor bastard can't swim!" He answered with a grin. (Strange breed those bikers.) Soon after the season came to an end and we sadly packed our gear up and said our farewells to our new friends and workmates we had been with for the past eleven weeks we had been on the Isle of Man, before boarding the ferry for home.

Chapter Twenty-Three
Ireland Again

We only had three days to relax before we had another tour of Ireland. Having seen what it was like on our previous visit none of us were particularly keen on going back, but the money was good and if we kept ourselves to ourselves, we reckoned we'd be okay.

Our digs had been upgraded to a very nice hotel and spa on the outskirts of Belfast. For a free gig we would have free bed and breakfast on the complex. The owner was quite a young guy who wasted no time telling us that he was a fierce loyalist. The hotel had started out as a small concern and because of his beliefs, he would accommodate private functions for the police, loyalist organisations, etc.

It didn't take long for the I.R.A. to notice this and they responded by blowing up a part of the hotel, killing a few people in the process. Somehow, the insurance was paid out and with the money, he rebuilt and added an extension. The I.R.A. returned a year or so later and blew it up again and after that a further extension was added. He now lived as a marked man but this didn't seem to faze him. (Well, not that I noticed anyway.)

Eddie was definitely keeping us busy while we were over there as there were no nights off on the whole tour. One of the gigs I remember with particular anxiety was a show up the Crumlin road where a barracks was stationed. Being a predominately Catholic area, this was not the safest of places to be. One local took great pleasure in telling us that vehicles with British number plates were regarded as army and would sometimes have car engines thrown down on them from the high-rise flats above.

Arriving at the base unscathed (apart from the very sweaty seats,) two massive steel doors swung open to let us in. The place felt like an outpost you would see in the cavalry/Indian movies. The officer in charge told us that sadly, they had lost a man that week on patrol in the area. This was said in a matter of fact way as it had become a fairly regular occurrence.

The show done, it was time for us to return to the safety of our digs (if they hadn't been blown up in our absence!) We were told that there was sometimes I.R.A. snipers up in the flats late at night and to make a beeline for the traffic lights farther down the road where it was deemed safe after that.

"How fast can your van go?" I was asked. (Me driving again!)

"Oh, about nought to sixty in two days." I replied.

"Hmm, well I'll have to get some guys to drive alongside you to shield you, cos as soon as you are through them gates it's foot down and arse to the wind."

We waited for a few minutes for our escort to arrive, me revving the engine to make sure it wouldn't conk out. A mini car pulled up alongside of us with two armed squaddies inside. You could tell by their expression that they would rather be anywhere else than there at that moment.

Before I could tell anyone that the escort was no use, as I was looking down at them and my cab was in no way protected, the gates were flung open and we were yelled at to get moving. The mini shot off, leaving our poor old van in its wake. It was then I noticed that I was all alone in the cab as everyone else was lying on the floor in the back! Halfway to the traffic lights the mini was on its way back to safety, having followed their orders to get to the lights, then return.

Meanwhile, I was trying to make myself as small as possible in the driver's seat, cursing the van for its lack of power. What seemed like an eternity to me we finally passed those damned lights and I pulled in to the side of the road, shaking like a leaf.

"Well that wasn't so bad," said Gordon, climbing out from under the rear seats, oblivious to the look of hate thrown from me in his direction.

Halfway through the tour we moved digs to a hotel in Lurgen where we were told there was a large catholic population in the town. The previous year someone had exploded a bomb in the main area of the town. This made us very aware of the position we were in. The barman in the hotel was a lovely guy named Dermot who was invaluable in telling us the right and wrong thing to do in the area. He also told us that quite a few members of the I.R.A. drank at the bar, and as we were playing a few army bases, to keep quiet about it for our own safety.

The second night staying there we arrived back to find the bar packed with drinkers.

"How'd it go then boys?" Dermot called over from behind the bar.

"Great!" I beamed, "the sergeants were a great crowd, and they gave us a slap up meal in their mess." The bar which had been very noisy with chatter suddenly became deadly silent and a crowd of hostile faces turned their attention toward me. I could see Dermot turn his eyes to the heavens in horror. In a moment of inspiration (or blind panic), I blurted out "can you guys not take a fucking joke!"

There was a second or two of further silence before one of the locals started laughing. This spread to the rest, who pointed at me and shook their heads as if to say what a real comic I was.

After the bar was closed, I was having a last drink of the night with Dermot. All he could repeatedly say was what a lucky bastard I was to still have my kneecaps intact.

Our last gig of the tour took us right down to the Ulster/Eire border which was seeing most of the trouble. The base was an old factory with the usual big gates and high walls added for security. As we drove through the gates we noticed a pile of wrecked cars and debris heaped up by the wall. We found out later that they'd had a mortar attack on the base only a few days before.

The guard motioned us to leave the vehicle for inspection. As they passed their detectors over the van, one of the team stiffened. "What's in the vehicle that shouldn't be?" He demanded.

"Only musical equipment." I replied.

"That's not what I'm reading here, I'm getting a sign that there are explosive materials inside." He said.

"Oh, that'll be the flash powder we use in the show." I answered. Suddenly, we were surrounded by soldiers with rifles pointed at us.

"You mean to tell me you have been driving all around Ulster with what basically is incendiary material and no one has stopped you!" Our guard screamed, "you're lucky it's us that found it otherwise it might have been someone who would shoot first and ask questions later!"

We had to empty out the van as the damn stuff was right at the back and once they were satisfied and had identified what it was, it was taken away and disposed of in a controlled explosion.

This meant we wouldn't have the same impact without the pyrotechnics, but it was better than being shot. We set up in the old works canteen which was quite a large area and also had a high stage built in it which was unusual for these shows.

With everyone gathered, the C.O. asked if he could say a few words before we started.

"As you know chaps, we've been under a bit of fire lately from the jolly old I.R.A. fellows, and although we don't expect any trouble tonight, as a precaution we have installed emergency drill procedures."

It was at this point that I happened to look up and notice that the place had a glass roof. (Not a lot of protection from incoming mortars, I thought.)

"Sections A,B, and C, will evacuate the room by the rear right hand door," the C.O. continued "while sections D, E, and F will exit by the rear left hand door, are there any questions?"

I put my hand up like a little schoolboy.

"Excuse me sir, what about the band?"

He looked puzzled for a moment. "Oh, hmm, well, just pick any door you like," was his answer.

Once the show was over the gear was packed in record time (it's amazing what fear can do) and once again a wave of relief swept over us all as we boarded the Larne ferry for home.

Chapter Twenty-Four
Isle of Man Again

As I stated previously, the 3,2,1, showcase had not quite taken us to the level of household fame that we had hoped for, but it had gotten us on the best venue circuit.

Our money per gig had improved considerably, but we were still not making as much as the other acts. Never the less it was great to be advertised alongside the likes of the Baron Knights, Frank Carson, Black Abbots and a whole host more who were all big names at the time.

Before we knew it, another year had passed and as we had had such a good season the previous year, we were booked at the Falcon Cliff for another summer season. Knowing what a great time we had had the previous year, we all looked forward to the eleven weeks in front of us.

Two weeks into the season I met someone who was to change my life in every way. We had finished our show and I'd gone to one of the hotels on the promenade to watch a later show. I had quite a lot to drink by the time it was my round and staggered up to the bar to be confronted with a beautiful girl serving there.

I gathered the drinks and as I was leaving the bar, I asked her for a date, which is not in my nature to do. She politely refused. When I asked why, she answered "you're drunk."

I apologised and left with the drinks. The next day, I couldn't get her out of my mind and that night I went back to her bar, (this time in a sober state) and asked her out again.

"No, you're too old for me," she said. This would normally put an end to my attempts, but inside a voice was telling me that I couldn't let her go. For the next few days I would be at her bar, where we talked more and more in between customers and realised we had quite a few things in common.

Eventually she agreed to meet me in her lunch hour the next day. Although we had less than an hour uninterrupted together, there was a spark between us and after that we began dating in earnest.

Things at home had steadily got worse and my wife and I practically lived separate lives, but this did not erase the guilt of not telling Tracey (my new love) I was still married.

Finally I could keep it a secret no longer, and after three weeks into our relationship, I had to come clean, even at the risk of losing her. I sat her down and blurted it all out, expecting her to storm out the door, but she just sat there quietly for a moment or two.

"Well," she sighed. "It's too late now isn't it?"

"Too late, how is it too late?" I asked.

"It's too late because I'm in love with you,

you old fart!" She answered. I jumped up and grabbed her, giving her a hug and a kiss, feeling as though I'd just won a million pounds.

"What do you mean old fart?" I said when I managed to calm down.

"Well, you are forty years old and I'm only twenty-four."

Funny, I'd never even thought about the age difference.

The rest of the season at the Falcon Cliff went by all too quickly and the time to pack and go home was upon us once more. The season had been another successful one for both our employers and ourselves.

The last night was a sombre affair for Tracey and I as she still had a contract to work for another six weeks at her hotel. We promised to phone each other every day and plan our way ahead, but before I left she said she wanted to phone her mother and tell her about us.

"I'll be very subtle and treat everything delicately when I explain things to her," she said. So, with my ear pressed against the phone, the following conversation took place.

"Hi mum, em, you know how you've always wanted me to settle down before I'm thirty, and meet a nice guy, well, I think I have."

"Oh, that's nice love, what's he like?"

"Well, he's Scottish (short pause at the other end.)

"Ah well, that's not so bad. What does he

do?"

"He plays in a band. "(A rather longer pause)

"What, for a living?"

"Yes mum, but they are really good."

"Okay?" Came the not so sure voice.

"He's a bit older than me."

"Oh, how much older dear?"

"About sixteen years." (A very long pause.)

"Oh, and one more thing, he's still married, love you mum, see you soon." And with that parting shot she put the phone down.

"Yeah Trace, that was subtle." I sighed.

Back in Scotland we began our circuit of clubs again and although Tracey and I talked every day we still missed each other terribly. There was a two-week run in the Yorkshire clubs and I would have two days break in between. Tracey had been home for a fortnight and had worked on softening her mum up for me, as I had managed to get transport over to see her.

It was with some apprehension on my part as I left Leeds late at night after the gig and headed towards Lancashire for my first visit to Tracey's house. She lived in a little village called Barrow, just outside Clitheroe, which took me longer to find than I had hoped. Having got lost about four times, it was four in the morning before I finally arrived and her mother had been in bed for hours.

As we quietly climbed the stairs to go to bed she told me to make myself some breakfast in the morning when I awoke, as she and her mum would be leaving early for work.

After a restful night I got up and went downstairs to make myself some toast. While the toast was in the toaster I went for a quick shower. On my way downstairs I noticed a flickering sort of light coming from the kitchen.

The toast had caught fire and there were flames licking up the kitchen cabinets. I frantically grabbed a tumbler and threw water on the fire, which caused the toaster to explode, fusing the whole house. Within seconds the fire was out, but not before it had burnt and blistered the paintwork and charred the walls on a good section of the kitchen.

With shaking hands (which had a few blisters from trying to put the damn fire out,) I picked up the phone and called Tracey at work.

"Trace I've set fire to your mum's kitchen."

"You've done what!" She shrieked. "How the hell did you manage to do that?"

"Well, I just put some bread in the toaster." I told her.

"You didn't leave it in, did you?" She interrupted me. "Cos it doesn't pop up, so you have to watch it and take it out when it's ready. I'll have to phone mum and tell her what's happened, she'll go ballistic, she only decorated the kitchen last month!"

So, there I was, in deep trouble with a woman I had still to meet and who wasn't exactly favourable towards me in the first place. (How to make friends and influence people.)

The first meeting that night was a strained affair as her mother viewed the blackened wall of her kitchen and destroyed toaster. In my defence I argued that a pop-up toaster should pop-up, but this was received with a steely glare and Tracey behind her, shaking her head and mouthing me to leave the subject alone. The following day I managed to buy a new toaster (one that popped up when it was told!) and found a decorator to repair the kitchen so that when they arrived home, everything was back to normal (apart from my finances.)

This seemed to build some bridges and Tracey's mother mellowed considerably. That night Tracey decided to take me on a pub crawl in the village which I thought was a bit strange as there were only two pubs there and they were so close to each other that they shared the same car park. Before heading there, we went to meet her brother Brett and his wife Karen. They had already heard about the escapade with the toaster, so I was determined to put up a better show and not let Tracey down again.

"We're in the kitchen." I heard her brother shout as we entered the house. The door to the kitchen was a two-part unit like a stable door and as I pushed the top half it came away from its hinges and clattered to the floor. I stood mortified as both Brett and Karen gave me a silent icy stare.

"I'm sorry, I, I, I, just pushed it and it fell off!" I spluttered. Brett rose slowly from his chair and walked menacingly towards me. Now, this was a big lad, in height and build, and I thought I was heading for a hammering. He thrust his face about two inches from my quivering continence and suddenly burst out laughing.

"Hi, I'm Brett," he chuckled. "Pleased to meet you, by the way that door has been broken for ages."

That was the first time he pulled a practical joke on me and it wasn't to be the last. (Many, many times over the years).

Having spent a pleasant couple of hours getting to know them both we headed for the first pub. As we entered we were greeted by the landlord Bill.

"Eh up Trace, is this your new boyfriend?" He asked. (In a small village news gets around fast and everyone also knew about the damn toaster!)

Tracey nodded to him. "By eck, he's a bit older than you, ain't he? Anyway, nice to meet you, where are you from?" He asked.

"I'm from Scotland." I told him. The welcoming outstretched hand was immediately withdrawn.

"I bloody hate jocks!"

Hmm, I thought to myself, welcome to the pleasant little village of Barrow!

As things happened, I got to know Bill very well over the years and we became good friends. (Good Scottish public relations from this lad!)

We sat down for our first drink.

"Come on slowcoach, it's time to move on," cried Tracey.

I gulped down my drink and we walked fifteen yards up the road to the other pub. I had barely got my second pint when it was time to go back to the first pub again. This went on the whole night with barely any time in between drinks, so by the end of the night I was a slobbering wreck.

As I fell into the hallway of the house, giggling like a schoolgirl, Tracey's mother stood with arms folded.

"What time is he leaving in the morning?" Was all she said as she climbed the stairs to bed. (The bridge building I had done with her had definitely come undone again.)

All too soon it was time to go and meet up with the band to continue our tour. (Hooray me thinks from her mother!) But the short time I had spent there had made me fall in love even more with Tracey and the area she lived in.

For the next few months, whenever I had a break, no matter how short, I would try to get there to see her (and mend things with her mum.)

Time seemed to fly by and before I knew it we were back on our way to the Isle of Man for what would be our last season there. Although I had not seen Tracey for over two months, she was there, waiting at the dock when we arrived, and it was as if we had just left each other only hours before.

It's time to mention Dulcie, Tracey's friend from her village, who had come over to work with her. She was a few years younger than Tracey and really knew how to enjoy her season. She arrived at the start, fresh faced and ready to go, and as the season progressed, the dark shadows under her eyes began to grow. This was not unexpected as she would burn the candle at both ends (and the middle as well.)

Many a morning she would be serving breakfast with a massive hangover, or still drunk (which she hid very well.) Tracey despaired of her, but we loved her anyway and wouldn't change her for the world. Anyway, there was a band called Bobby Socks at another venue on the island and Dulcie had fallen head over heels in love with Keith who was playing bass for them.

My first impressions of him were far from favourable as he seemed like bit of a poser, driving up and down the esplanade in his jeep with private number plates. Both Tracey and I tried to warn her off, but Dulcie would not have any of it. As time would tell, Tracey and I were totally wrong about him and Keith came to live in Clitheroe later and became a close friend and fellow band member.

The season went as well as the previous two and we happily slipped into the summer routine. My brother Tom (who I have not mentioned so far, and you will see why as I continue) had decided to come over for a week with my sister-in-law Heather.

Now, Tom was regarded as a bit of a character back home (an understatement) and I was always the quiet one in the family. He had been a bit of a jack the lad in his younger days, much to the disapproval of my dad, so it was with a bit of apprehension on my part as I met him off the ferry.

Tom, being Tom, knew most of the island in the first two days and it was strange to walk down the streets with him with everyone greeting him with friendly "hello's" and "hiya Tam," like he had lived there all his life.

At breakfast one morning he said, "what's the best golf course on the island?"

I told him that Peel golf club was the best but you near enough had to be a lawyer and above as it was very exclusive.

"Right, get your clubs and meet me at the car," he said. No amount of reasoning from me would change his mind, and although I kept telling him he was just wasting his time, off we set for Peel. Tom was an avid golfer and was honorary house captain of the old course Musselburgh, which had the distinction of being the oldest course in the world. (Not club, but course, for all you golf fans). Getting out of the car at the car park at Peel he donned his house captain's blazer with the old course badge and said, "you wait in the car, I'll just have a word with someone in the club."

I had resigned myself to a fruitless journey back to Douglas, when five minutes later, the president of the club came over to the car with Tom, apologising that the club professional couldn't be available to take us around the course but hoped we would enjoy our game, free of charge of course.

"How the hell did you manage that?" I asked. Tom just winked and motioned me to get the clubs out of the car. There was a large crowd gathering at the first tee which made me very nervous as I'm one of the worst golfers in the world. (Never below twenty-eight handicap.)

Tom teed off with a beautiful shot, straight down the middle of the fairway. Then it was my turn. Thwack! Ten yards into the rough on the right-hand side.)

The crowd made a low muttering sound with a few politely clapping. Thwack! (a little farther, but onto the opposite green.)

This time there were a few titters from the crowd and a lot more muttering.

Thwack! (Fifty yards, but narrowly missing the muttering crowd on the way.)

As we walked up to where our balls were the crowd had decided that they had seen enough and gone back to the clubhouse.

"Tom, what did you say to the President?" I asked.

"Oh," he said casually, "I told him you were the old course professional."

I could have battered him over the head with one of my clubs at that moment. After the game we went into their clubhouse for a drink. Tom was the centre of attention, while I sat alone like a leper in the corner with only a few glances and shaking of the heads from some of the members.

Tom and heather enjoyed the rest of their week and all too soon it was time for them to go home, but not before he had another of his moments.

On the morning they were leaving they had not made it down for breakfast and the ferry was leaving shortly. I finally roused him by banging loudly on his door.

"Tam, you're going to miss the ferry!" I cried.

"No problem, I'll be down in a minute." He replied. By the time they both appeared the ferry was due to leave.

"You're going to have to catch the next one!" I told him.

"Nah, we'll make it." Said Tom confidently, as he threw the bags onto the back seat of the car, got Heather safely seated and shot off like a bullet.

Everyone in the hotel agreed that he would be back shortly, as we could hear the ferry blasting its horn for departure. Not long after we saw the ferry pull out of the harbour. I waited for a while to greet him back but there was no sign of him.

Finally, thinking he may have broken down or was waiting by the quayside, I went in search of him. As I approached the terminal I overheard the policeman on duty telling his partner how this maniac driver had screamed up to the ferry as it was pulling away from the jetty, and like a stunt driver, sailed over the gap and landed on the ship's deck. I quietly turned around and left before anyone recognised that I was his brother.

All too soon the season was over and we would be heading back to the mainland to continue our circuit of clubs and nightclubs. It was a sad final evening as Tracey and I visited all our usual haunts to say goodbye to everyone. Tracey still had a month to work on her contract before she headed home, but we had decided that we could not be parted anymore and that I would tell my wife that it was all over between us.

We had nothing planned as to how we

were going to get together as she was in England and I was in Scotland, but we were adamant that we would find a way.

So, once again, it was with a heavy heart, and a great deal of apprehension for what was ahead of me in the coming days that I watched that beautiful island disappear from view.

Chapter Twenty-Five
New Beginnings

The showdown with my wife came off better than I had anticipated as she informed me that she had met someone else while I was away. We both felt a sense of relief as the sham of our marriage was finally over. Although this made it easy for us, we knew it wouldn't be so easy for the kids. (It's always them that suffer the most.)

I had made up my mind that I would make a clean break of it as soon as I finished the forthcoming tour of Belfast which was only days away.

It turned out to be one of the worst days of my life, as I had to sit the kids down to tell them I was leaving. The gravity of the situation hit home hard as I found myself in my old room, at my parent's house. I had come full circle. The only bright light on the horizon was Tracey, who was in constant contact with me throughout that dark time, helping me to adjust and cope with the upheaval.

My folks couldn't have been more helpful as they knew things between my wife and I had not been right for a very long time and were there to give me support. The first time they were introduced to Tracey, they took to her immediately, which was a huge weight off both our minds.

Tracey had decided that it would be best

if she moved to Scotland to be with me, so I began hunting for a place for us. It came in the shape of a dilapidated farmhouse cottage in the middle of nowhere. The nearest road was almost two miles away and the nearest village was three. We didn't have much money, so the rent of ten pounds a week was about as much as we could manage. My dad came with me to look it over, and as soon as I walked through the door my heart sank. The lounge ceiling had a huge hole in it where it had collapsed and the birds had got in through the roof, leaving bird droppings and feathers everywhere, as well as leaves and twigs which were strewn all over every room.

My dad saw my face.

"Not to worry, I'll soon have it licked into shape," he said. As I was getting ready for another three-week tour I had my doubts, especially when I couldn't be there to help.

"You just get on with your gigs and leave it up to me," he said cheerfully. "You won't recognise the place when you get back!" He added.

As I drove off the following day, I had my misgivings. I need not have worried. On my return, dad and I drove up to the cottage and when he opened the door I was amazed at the transformation. The ceiling and roof had been fixed, both ceiling and walls were freshly painted. They had found chairs, a settee, a bed, carpets, and even a television. It was perfect. Looking at my dad with a big grin on his face, I could have kissed him for the super human effort he, my mum, and brother had put in to make that cottage a home.

Tracey was over the moon when I told her, and on Christmas Eve, nineteen eighty-seven, we moved in and started our new life together. At first it was working out just fine for the two of us. When we toured Tracey came along with us and she was no problem as she blended in well with the rest of the guys.

After a few months the band dropped a bombshell on us. They had had a vote behind our backs and thought that Tracey shouldn't really come on tour with us as they had to watch how they behaved when she was around. This was a joke as far as I was concerned, as they swore and farted as if she wasn't there anyway.

Bobby had slowly but surely over time, asserted control over the rest of the band members and I was certain he was behind it, as we were disliking each other more and more, and this was a way of getting at me. At this point my dislike turned to a smoldering hatred, and I regarded the rest of the band with a newfound mistrust.

This new rule meant that every time I was away, I would stock the cottage up with provisions and leave poor Tracey on her own in the middle of nowhere with only a telephone to contact the outside world. As she couldn't drive she was virtually a prisoner in the cottage until I came home. The band knew that this would be what would happen, which made me angry to think they could be so uncaring.

Sometimes, when we could afford it, I would send her home to her mother for a visit, but those times were few and far between. How my darling put up with it I will never know, but as I look back on it now, she must have loved me very much to endure those dark times.

The eighties were coming to an end and the band were doing the same old circuits as we had done for the last two years, with no major breakthrough into the big time. If anything, under Bobby's influence, the off-stage behaviour of the band was becoming more and more of an embarrassment to me as their antics was to say the least, less than professional. The more I complained about the behaviour, the more of a rift between myself and the rest of the band grew, which Bobby nurtured as much as he could.

In May of nineteen eighty-nine Tracey asked me if I would consider moving down to Lancashire as there was a chance of a house there. As the band was travelling up and down the length and breadth of the whole of the United Kingdom I thought it was a great idea, especially as she would have her family and friends close by.

"Good, I've got one," she said gleefully.

She had already done the donkey work and had a place lined up! I often wonder what she would have done if I had said no. Within two weeks we had moved to our little house in the middle of Clitheroe and I could see by the look on Tracey's face what a happy move it was for her.

Things with the band and myself had deteriorated to the extent that I dreaded going on tour with them, and even more, spending time in their company. We had landed a season at Thorpe Park amusement centre. Our venue was the theatre in the middle of the complex. We were booked for six half an hour shows per day, from Monday to Saturday. The money was ludicrously low (it worked out about twenty pounds a show.) It was supposed to give us exposure to higher things, but I had my doubts (and I was proved right in the end.)

Incredibly, the rest of the guys thought it was a great move. The money was so low that we would have to work in the London clubs at night, after the six shows at the park to make a decent wage. Considering we had played the top venues in the London area such as the Lakeside Country Club, Rifles and the like, this felt to me like a major step backwards.

Things went from bad to worse when we arrived for the first shows. It appeared that there were some safety issues with the theatre and we would have to do our show in the fast food area until it was resolved.

And so it was, we put on our show to the sound of knives and forks scraping on plates, kids running around screaming, throwing burgers and hot dogs on the stage. The noise was so deafening we could barely hear our instruments. Tracey could see how desperately unhappy I was on my brief visits home.

"Listen love, do you really want to carry on like this?" She asked me bluntly. I shook my head and told her I had almost had enough of the whole thing.

"Right, because if you want, my brother's mate is looking for someone to work for him in his electrical firm. If you really want to give up on the band, I'll arrange a meeting with him."

There and then I felt as though a great weight had been lifted off from my shoulders. I finally had a chance to get out of the miserable existence that had dragged me down for the past few years.

True to her word, Tracey arranged the meeting with Dave the boss and I was offered the job. It wasn't due to start for another month which gave me time to hand my notice in to the band.

"You can't go!" Shouted Adam when I told them of my leaving. "We'll need more time than that!" Pleaded Gordon.

"Well, for the last few years Bobby has

always said that I would be the easiest member to replace, so here's your chance." I replied smugly.

"You're just trying to fuck the band up!" Snarled Bobby.

"You started doing that a long time ago, you fat bastard!" I retorted. "Anyway, I'm going for lunch, anyone coming?" Four faces stared at me as I ambled out of the room feeling on top of the world as I finally got my revenge for all the hard times they had put me through.

As the time drew nearer to my departure they tried every trick in the book to make me stay until my replacement was ready.

"You do realise you are under contract?" Alan said.

"Nope, I'm not under contract, the band is." I answered.

"Well if you think you are getting any money back for the van or the gear, that ain't gonna happen," said Gordon.

"Don't give a shit, it'll be worth it to get away from you bunch of bastards." It felt great to say exactly what I felt after having to hold it in for so long.

Just before the end, we were booked to headline a showcase in Central London. There were five acts apart from us. All the acts were using our PA system, so we had arrived early. As I was in charge of setting up the pyrotechnics I was left on my own while the others went for lunch. The duo who were third on the bill turned up.

This duo had had a major hit in the charts a few years earlier, but it was a "one-hit-wonder." (They were so famous I can't remember their name.)

"Hoi! Hoi!" One of them shouted.

Being rudely distracted from what I was doing, I snapped back, "what do you want?"

"Let's have the PA on, we want to do a sound-check." He demanded.

"I'm a bit busy just now, mate." I said.

"Never mind being busy, turn the fucking PA on now," he snarled back.

Being in no mood to argue, I went across to the mixing desk and switched it on, satisfied that I had followed orders to the letter. They headed for the exit. Just before they left, the one who had been giving me a hard time turned to me and said, "with your attitude, that is why you are just a roadie, a gofer, and I am an artiste."

The evening went well and all the acts, (including the artistes) went down very well with the audience. It was then our turn to finish the show. As all the acts had stayed around to watch us, it was a treat to see the "artiste's" face when the curtains drew back and he saw me.

After the show in the hospitality room, I made a beeline for him. "With your attitude, that is why you are a support act, and we are top of the bill." I gleefully informed him. (There's an old saying that you should be nice to people on the way up, because you will probably meet them on the way down.)

It seemed like time was dragging on but finally the last day came, and then the last show. As I folded my stage suit ready to hand over I couldn't help but let out a hoop of delight. (Very unprofessional, but who fucking cared!) I could see it in their eyes that they still couldn't believe I was going through with it. Here he was, good old dependable Brick, who never spoke back or caused any bother, walking out on the band he had started nineteen years earlier.

It was a deliriously happy chappie that loaded his gear, swearing never to set eyes on those guys ever again and headed north, home to be with his darling Tracey.

Chapter Twenty-Six
The Normal Life

Tracey was worried that after years in the "limelight" so to speak, I would find it hard to adjust to a nine-to-five job, but as far as I was concerned it was just what I needed at that moment.

The assurance of a steady wage coming in every week and knowing that your weekends were free to do as you pleased, was like a new world to me. Coupled by the fact that I really enjoyed the job, life was pretty good.

A few months passed in this way and then I began to get the urge to play again, though not as a full job but as a hobby. Tracey (God bless her) was behind me all the way and encouraged me to give it a go. Tracey's best friend Rachel and her husband Tim had become close friends with me. Tim could play guitar a bit and he suggested we try out as a duo. This seemed like a good idea, so I agreed.

After a few weeks of rehearsals in the house I reckoned we were good enough to go out on the road. We scraped together some old amps and speakers I had gathered over the years, bought some backing tracks to give us a drum and keyboard fill-in and we were ready. When I say ready I forgot to mention the cabinets we had to build to house our main vocal speakers. Tim had found some wood that would do for the job.

Unfortunately the wood was cast off work tops in brilliant white, so when we fixed our black coloured speakers into the newly built cabinets they looked like washing machines! (As they say, beggars can't be choosers.)

As The Mimics had travelled throughout the U.K. and abroad I had a few contacts to phone for bookings. We settled on an agent who was local and would give us decent venues. On our first gig Tim was a nervous wreck as he had never performed in public before.

I didn't want to worry him, but I was quite nervous myself as I had never taken the roll of the lead singer before. We had expected a small venue, being as how this was our first gig and completely unknown to the local club scene. When we arrived, my jaw dropped. The place was huge, and even by Mimic's standards, it was a top club. Trying hard not to let Tim see that I was shaking like a leaf, we took to the stage.

I don't know if it was adrenaline, or luck, or both, but we went down really well, which pleased me all the more, as the venue obviously had a high standard in entertainment. Nervous as he was, Tim came through with flying colours and no one noticed him shaking more than me from behind his mic stand.

In high spirits, and the happiest I had been as a performer for many a year, we set off home to tell Rachel and Tracey, who were waiting anxiously to hear all about it.

The following months saw our little duo take off on the club circuit and every weekend was taken up with gigging around Lancashire. "Leyland and Hart" as we were called, were becoming quite sought after and I wondered, that after trying so hard, and nearly making it with The Mimics, my chance had come again to make it big.

All went well for a while but I began to notice a change coming over Tim. I think he began to realise that it was not all a bed of roses and basically, your time was not your own at the weekends. He began to grumble about the venues, travelling, the money, etc and I could see the end in sight for us both.

I could see his side of the story as I had done this for almost thirty years and I considered it the norm, whereas it was all new to him. We both liked a drink and even though I did all the driving (again) meaning Tim could have a few when we were playing, and I had to abstain, it still didn't make up for the weekend all day sessions that he enjoyed now and then.

The final nail in the coffin came one Saturday when I went to pick him up for the gig. He had been out drinking with Keith (who had moved to Clitheroe by this time) and it was obvious that he was very drunk. Keith, who was not much better, thought this was hilarious. (I still haven't forgiven him!)

With no time to cancel I managed to load the gear up and pour him into the car.

"Just try and get through the night will you?" I pleaded. This fell on deaf ears as the sound of snoring could be heard from the passenger's seat. Dear God! I thought, if I could prop him up and make some excuse to the club, I might get away with it. As we turned into the club car park Tim awoke with a start, asking if we were there yet. It's going to be ok, I thought to myself as he seemed to have sobered up a lot.
I left him in the car while I set up the gear and let him sober up a bit more.

I went back to the car to take him to the dressing room. Oh no! no Tim! Where the hell had he disappeared to? I had visions of him wandering aimlessly through the streets.

I needn't have worried. As I went back into the club, there he was, propping up the bar with a pint in his hand.

"What the fuck are you doing?" I hissed.

"Iss all right," he slurred. "I'm juss getting a bit of Dutch courage."

"Fuck the Dutch courage, you're pissed!" I raged. (It's a known fact that you never tell a drunk that he is drunk.)

"I am not!" He replied indignantly "I've just had a couple and a wee bit tired," and as if to prove a point, he ordered another beer. I pleaded with him to make that his last until we got home and he grudgingly agreed.

We got through the first set with just a few mistakes that no one seemed to notice and I began to relax a little. I shouldn't have let my guard down, as just before the second set Tim was back at the bar. There was no hiding the fact that he was drunk this time as he staggered on to the stage. Most of the committee were staring at us and shaking their heads. I was praying to God, Buddha, anyone, just to get through the rest of the night, but my prayers fell on deaf ears.

Half way through the set Tim decided that he wanted to dance and jumped off the stage and began gyrating along with the music. Unfortunately, with only the drum machine and my bass guitar, there wasn't much of a melody, but Tim didn't seem to mind as he moved to and fro. After many requests over the mike from me and a lift back on to the stage by some of the very bemused audience Tim took up his position and we hacked our way through the set to the bitter end.

Once I had packed the gear in the car and managed to hustle Tim out of the club (who by this time was sleeping like a baby in the passenger seat) I returned to face the wrath of the officials who told me we would never play in their club again and cut our fee by half.

When we reached home, I woke Tim out of his drunken slumber to give him his share.

"What's this, you're thirty quid short?"

He said. I told him I would come round in the morning to sort it out as I was in no mood to argue after what had gone on. The next day we sat down to thrash things out and agreed to call it a day as a duo, but still stay friends. With Tim telling me that he had lost his appetite for playing a while before, it worked out well between us.

Chapter Twenty-Seven
Lost Love

I was left in a bit of a dilemma as our duo had almost a full diary. Salvation came in the form of Keith, who I found out wasn't really a bass player, but a very accomplished guitarist he saw my problem and offered to step in and help with the gigs and as he knew most of the numbers, we were ready by the next booking.

Tim and I had a great many of our songs on backing tracks. Keith, being a much more experienced player, insisted we get the music written down so we could use the clubs backing bands, which were normally keyboards and drums. This was a good idea as then it would be authentic and leave no doubts about what was on tape or what was actually being played by us.

Using club backing was also a bit of a gamble as some of the resident musicians were good and some quite frankly were awful. The trouble was that every club would tell you they had the best backing band in the land. They were normally local lads who were part and parcel of the club as well, so it was unwise to criticise them.

The discovered that the best thing to do when we got a bad outfit was to crank up the guitars and drown them out. Keith had a pet hate for club organists as most didn't follow the music we had written for them. This would get his dander up and he would inform them in no uncertain terms where their organ was going to go if they didn't play what was written in black and white in front of them!

One night in particular comes to mind. We were playing in Blackpool and in the first set the organist was not only playing his own interpretation of our songs but was so loud that we couldn't even hear our own guitars. Looking over at Keith I could see him staring at this noisy impresario, and his mood darkening by the minute.

"Look mate," Keith shouted, back in the privacy of the dressing room. "Just play what we've written down for you, not what the fuck you want to play!"

The keyboard player started to say that he thought he could improve on the music when Keith nipped him in the bud.

"That's the way we do it, and that's the way it's been proven many times and while we are at it, drop the volume 'cos I can't hear fuck all but you banging away!"

The organist slunk out of the room, and the drummer, who had witnessed it all, burst out laughing.

"He's had that coming for a while," he said. "Thinks he's god's gift to music, I'm glad you took the bastard down a peg or two!"

The second set started in a strained atmosphere but at least the keyboard player was playing as he should, and at a reasonable volume. Just when we thought it was resolved we noticed the volume increasing ever so slightly with every number until it was almost as loud as it had been in the first set.

Eventually Keith could take no more, and at the end of a particularly loud intrusion, Keith casually walked over to where the organ was plugged into the wall and ripped the wire out of the socket. Handing the open-mouthed organist the cable with the bare wires dangling at the end, he walked back to the mike and introduced our next number.

This did not go down well with our keyboard player, who scurried off the stage to tell the committee what had happened. On finishing the set (and receiving two encores) we returned to the dressing room to find it full of committee members (and one upset organist) demanding compensation for the wilful damage. (about one pound fifty by my reckoning.)

"Take it out of our money, and while you're at it get a new organist because he is shit!" Shouted Keith.

Needless to say, we never played that club again.

On the whole drummers were much easier to get on with. I could never understand why, on average, the organists were paid far more than them as they were just as important as far as I was concerned. But, as you can guess, there I always one or two who make you lose faith in them. An instance that stands out in my mind was a gig in Manchester.

As we set up, I noticed on one of the drummers stands there was what looked like a milkman's bottle carrier attached to it. It was firmly bolted on, so it was definitely a permanent fixture. Both Keith and I wondered what this was for as we couldn't see any purpose for it on the drumming side.

The answer soon became clear as the backing duo took to the stage to start the night. The drummer had his hands full with a tray of six pints of beer which he placed carefully in the compartments of the milk holder. After the end of their first music spot there were six empty pint pots in the holder. Our percussionist casually placed the empty pints onto the tray and headed to the bar for a refill. As we were on in about five minutes after we were slightly alarmed to think how he was going to play. He returned with the tray which held only three pints on it this time. "

Got to keep my wits about me," he said. "Can't be drinking too much during the cabaret spot."

The spot went well, and to both Keith and my surprise he performed quite well. Back to the bar went our intrepid musician and returned with six more pints.

"It's only the dance spot now, so I can

relax a bit," he informed us. His idea of relaxing ended up a harrowing experience for us, as the vast amount of alcohol taken in a short period of time quickly began to take its toll.

He was sitting (slouching) with glazed eyes behind his drums and generally hitting out at any drum he could focus on at the time, which wasn't very often. The organist just looked at us with a "it's always like this," look and manfully carried on. Near the end of this shambles I was thanking the crowd, when from behind came this shout.

"Hey, hey!"

I carried on, trying to ignore the drunken idiot behind me.

"Hey you!" I had no option but to break off talking to the audience and turn to see what was wrong.

"Pass us them pints will you, mate?" He slurred, pointing to the six pints on a tray at the edge of the stage.

The bookings kept coming in and with my electrical job as well, things were looking good. As I arrived home one evening Tracey was sitting on the sofa with a strange look on her face. I'd seen that face before many years ago.

"Bloody hell, your pregnant aren't you?" I cried. She had been coaxing me for ages to have a child and I had given in only a short time before.

"You're not mad are you?" She asked,

with a pleading look on her face.

"Well, it looks like we are going to be parents then!" I said.

So there was I, forty five years old and stepping back into fatherhood again.

"There's one thing though," I demanded. "It had better be a girl, because I've got my quota of boys!"

And so, it was that nine months later my beautiful daughter Becky was born.

Tracey had given up her job and even with the duo and electrical work, money was tight as we now had a mortgage on the house, but life was moving in the right direction.

It was only a few months later when Tracey began to feel unwell. Several visits to the doctor only concluded that as she'd had a difficult birth, it would take time for her to get back to full fitness again.

As the months went by with no improvement she was finally sent for tests. A week after, we were called in to the hospital for the results. It appeared there was a blood disorder and an operation would be needed to remove her spleen.

This hit us like a thunderbolt as we were expecting a course of tablets or something similar to rectify the problem. The day of the operation came, and when I was allowed into the ward to see her, I rushed to her bedside. She was still heavily sedated and I held her hand

and whispered encouraging words to her to try and comfort her, saying things like, "it's all over now love, I'll soon have you home."

A senior nurse appeared and in a very brisk manner, addressed Tracey.

"Tracey, Tracey, can you hear me?" She called. Tracey, though still in her sedated state nodded.

"We've found something a bit more serious during the operation dear."

Not waiting for an answer, she strode off. I sat by the bed, stunned, what was going on? Five minutes later she returned.

"Tracey, when I say we've found something serious, what do you think that means?"

Tracey, still under the influence of the anaesthetic muttered something about more operations.

"No Tracey, there will be no more operations," she said. Tracey came to a bit more with the news.

"Do you mean I might die?" She whispered.

"Yes," was all the nurse said, before leaving the room once more.

Stunned and shocked as I was, I ran after her and demanded to know what was going on.

"The doctor who performed the operation will be here presently to explain everything," she said.

I went back to the room in a daze to see Tracey weeping uncontrollably. As I held her in my arms I couldn't find any words to say to comfort her and all I could do was cry along with her. The surgeon came in ten minutes later, and by the look on his face it was as bad as I was hoping it would not be.

"Tracey I'm afraid it's cancer. We've found it in your liver and unfortunately it has spread, there's no way to soften the blow I'm afraid, but we will wait for the biopsy result and see what can be done," he said.

I will always remember the look on Tracey's face as she bravely looked at the surgeon and asked in a clear voice, "am I going to die?"

The surgeon dropped his eyes. "Yes, I'm afraid so, I'm so sorry."

"How long have I got?" She asked again. "You could have two years, maybe longer, we don't know for certain until the results are back," he answered.

"And when will that be?" She persisted.

"We'll have them by Christmas Eve but we can hold them over until after the year if you want?" Came his reply.

Tracey took a deep breath and said, "no, as soon as the results are here I want to know."

When he left the room we both sat in silence, holding hands for what seemed an age. All too soon it was time for me to leave to look after Becky. As I looked back, seeing her looking out of the window, her face showing the gravity of what had just unfolded; I had to rush down the corridor as the tears welled up in me again.

I cried all the way home. Why? Why? I kept asking myself. We had made plans for the future, keeping in mind the age difference of sixteen years between us, and had always assumed that I would be the one to die first. By the time I arrived home I had composed myself and then began the painful duty of informing all the families and friends.

As promised, the results arrived on Christmas Eve and hoping against hope, we turned up for the meeting with the surgeon. There was no miracle that a mistake had been made. It was confirmed she had terminal cancer. Words by the surgeon telling us that treatment was available which might delay the inevitable, and that new advances were being discovered all the time, mainly fell on deaf ears as we sat in silence, realising the finality of it.

As I looked across at my love on Christmas Day, helping our little Becky open her presents, laughing and smiling throughout, I was amazed how brave she was, knowing that she might not see another. Once or twice during the day I caught her wistfully looking out of the window in an unguarded moment and my heart was torn to pieces.

As if by an ironic coincidence I had had a

dispute with my employer and had quit my job only a few weeks before. This left me free to look after Tracey as best I could. Chemotherapy had been prescribed and the treatment was started almost immediately after the new year.

As anyone having gone through it can confirm, it is an aggressive and brutal treatment, and to watch her being so ill with the after effects for days after each course was heartbreaking for me.

In those situations we turned to any source of comfort and ideas to give us a glimmer of hope. This even included faith healing which actually made Tracey feel better. It was probably wishful thinking but if it gave her hope, then I was all for it.

As we moved into April of nineteen ninety-three the test results that were taken regularly were encouraging. It appeared the tumours had been halted, and though not in remission, hadn't spread any farther.

All this time Tracey had carried on with her life and never complained or got angry with her situation. Near the end of that month she asked if she could stay in bed that morning as she was in a bit more pain than usual. The Macmillan nurse was calling round that day so I knew she was in good hands.

When she came she suggested I take Tracey to the local hospice where she could be given something to ease her discomfort and check she was alright and I could pick her up the next day. As I dropped her off she kept reminding me of the list of things to do that day. I gave her a quick kiss and promised to take her to lunch the next day.

That night, with Becky fed, bathed, and tucked up in bed for the night I put my feet up and settled down to watch some television. At about ten-o-clock the phone rang. It was the hospice. Could I come in as soon as possible as Tracey was having difficulty breathing? I frantically phoned around to get someone to look after Becky, thankfully her friend Virginia and sister-in-law Karen were there in minutes.

Tracey's mum insisted on coming with me and we set off as fast as we could. As we entered the hospice we were shown into a side room. A deep foreboding came over us, and then the news. Tracey was gone. She had had a massive heart attack in her room and by the time the nurses had got to her she was dead. My wonderful, beautiful darling was dead.

Even though you prepare for this day the shock, disbelief, and grief hits you like a sledgehammer. We were shown into the room, and there she lay pale and cold. Within half an hour her brother Brett and father Brian, along with Brian's second wife Joyce were there.

We all sat around the bed comforting each other as best we could. So there it was, my lovely Tracey, mother of an eighteen month-old baby, whom she would never see growing up, was dead. She had just turned thirty-one years old.

I drove back home alone as Tracey's mum was being looked after by the rest of the family and half way there, in a quiet cul-de-sac, I stopped and shed another mountain of tears.

When I arrived home I talked briefly to Virginia and Karen and when they had gone home, I sat alone with my thoughts. I went up to Becky's room and sat by her cot. She looked so small and vulnerable lying there with her breathing so steady and a little smile on her face. I broke into tears again and tried to stifle my groans as I wondered what the future would hold for us now that our lives had been torn apart.

Chapter Twenty-Eight
Going Solo

The next few days went by in a blur.

As most people who have been in the same situation will agree, your mind is numb and you have so much to do planning the funeral that you haven't much time to grieve. When the day came I went through the motions in a zombie state and when the ordeal was over, I returned to an empty house to just sit and take it all in.

Tracey's mum had indicated that she would like to look after Becky during the week as she had retired, so that I could still find work and keep the duo going. This meant that I could have her at home in the evenings and she would also take her for the weekends to enable me to do the cabaret work if I wanted.

As much as I did not feel like continuing, she convinced me that it would be for the better, to get me focused on something and stop me thinking about Tracey all the time. And so, a few weeks later, Keith and I started gigging again. Not long after that Keith came by to tell me the bad news that he was having to go to Germany to work.

I phoned our agent to tell him and he suggested I go out on my own.

"But what about all the gigs in the diary for the duo?" I asked.

"Don't worry "came the casual reply, "just say your partner was taken ill and you didn't want to let them down, that way if you die on your arse, you might get a bit of sympathy." (Cheers for that.)

My first night as a solo act arrived and I was a nervous wreck. As soon as I walked on the stage, for some reason, I was calm and performed really well. It even surprised me!

It was a great feeling to get two encores at the end, and a promise of a rebooking. So started my solo career under the name of Brian Flockhart, dynamic vocalist, (the agent's words, not mine!) for the next three years.

It didn't take long to see, as a solo act, how you were treated in the clubs and pubs. On the whole, you were treated like a second-class citizen and of course the resident bands were a part of the attitude as well. (To those bands that treated me well, I apologise. But to the ones that didn't, you know who you are!)

The majority of the organists would flick through my music with a bored expression as if to say "same old shit," but I still went down well with the audience almost all the time, despite them messing up the simple music in front of them.

Getting back to the people in charge, (my pet bugbear!) on one occasion I was sent to a club in Wigan. I went to see the entertainments secretary (bus driver by day.)

"Hi, I'm your turn for tonight," holding my hand out in greeting.

"Three spots," was all he said.

"What?" I asked.

"I said three spots, you do three spots." Was his gruff reply.

"Hi, I'm Brian, how do you do?" I tried again.

"I told you three spots, do you understand, three spots!" He barked.

I withdrew my welcoming hand and headed back to the car to get my gear out.

"Hey! Are you any good?" He shouted.

"Who me, nah I'm shit."

"Just hold on their lad, leave your stuff where it is and come with me," he ordered.

He ushered me into his office (broom cupboard,) picked up the phone and dialled my agent. Just to make sure I heard everything being said, he put it on speaker mode.

"Hello," came my agent's voice.

"This club is the best club in the North West (how many times had I heard that?) and we will not accept bad acts here, and that lad you sent down tonight is shit!" He roared.

"But he's always gone down well everywhere else and never let me down?" He replied. There was a short pause, and he came back on the phone.

"Wait a minute, it's only seven-o-clock. Surely he hasn't been on yet?"

"No, he hasn't, but he told me he was shit, okay!" Came the reply.

The agent asked if he could talk to me in private with the speaker mode off.

"Listen!" He hissed down the line at me, "you are talking to a guy who thinks Sunday lunch is pie and fucking peas, don't try and be smart with pricks like this, now put me back on to him!"

I don't know what was said between them, but I was told that I was to go on for the first set.

"I'll be in the front row lad and if I go like this," chopping his fingers across his throat in a cutting motion, "I want you off!" My "entertainments official" said.

As I started my first spot, sure to his word, there he was, sitting right in the middle of the first row, ready to give me the "cut throat" sign. His face lightened up as I got farther into the set and he could see I was going down well with the crowd. At the break he followed me into the dressing room.

"That were alright, that," he said, grudgingly. "Where are you playing around Christmas?"

"Anywhere but this shit hole!" I replied. (This turned out to be a great way to get up certain people's noses and get sent home early!)

Another instance comes to mind (one of countless.) I was playing in Yorkshire, and as I was just about to go on stage, the drummer approached me.

"Don't carry on later than ten forty-five," he said. I found this very unusual as the normal time to finish was at eleven, with five minutes allowed for encores.

The organist came in. "Did he tell you ten forty-five?" He asked. I told him that I had got the message. "Cos if you go past that time you'll be standing up there on your own," he said. As no one else was at hand to tell me different I did as I was told and cut my final spot down to suit. My timing was perfect, and at ten forty-five on the dot we finished.

Without a word, the two of them covered their instruments with dust sheets with army precision and walked down the stage steps, out the fire escape door, across the car park, up the steps to the small railway platform, and boarded the train just as it was leaving. Now that is what I call timing!

One of the worst areas to work for me was Cumbria. (Barrow-in-Furness to narrow it down a bit.) I'm sure the residents of that town are very nice people as a whole, but I invariably got the small section that was definitely not cabaret friendly. (Maybe just me.)

The first instance I recall was playing the largest club in the town. (The name escapes me, thank God!) On arriving at the front door, I could see an old man with the compulsory cloth cap on head in his little cubicle inside the door. It was one of those clubs where you had to enter a code to gain access. After banging on the door and waving my arms like I was trying to park a jumbo jet for five minutes to get his attention, and being completely ignored, he laboriously hauled himself out of his seat and came across to face me through the glass window.

"Members only!" he barked.

"I'm your cabaret for tonight!" I shouted back.

"Eh?" he replied, screwing his face up and lifting a cupped hand to his ear. (Not only ignorant but bloody deaf as well! I thought.)

"I'm your turn!" I screamed.

"Go round the back!" He yelled, waving his arm in a multitude of directions.

"How do I get there!" I asked, still shouting to be heard through the triple glass. He gave me an exasperated look.

"Take the second left at the roundabout, turn right, second left again, left again, first left at that roundabout, first right, second left, left again, first left at that roundabout, second right, and I'll open the door for you."

This was rattled off at great speed and before I could ask him to repeat the instructions, he shuffled back to his little cubicle and continued to ignore me.

Half an hour later, having got lost countless times and driven up and down almost every street in the damn town, I finally found the club's elusive back door.

"Where the fuck have you been, I've been standing here for ages, I've got other things to do you know!" My genial doorman screamed.

"I just got a little bit lost," I replied sarcastically.

"Lost, how the hell did you get lost, everybody round here knows where the back door is!" He cried. The fact that I wasn't from "round there" seemed to escape his mind.

Biting my tongue, I decided to keep quiet and asked him where the stage was. A wry grin came over his face.

"Right, you go along this corridor till you reach the end, up two flights of stairs, then come back on yourself through the second door, and the stage is at the far end of the hall."

Looking at his smug face at that instant I contemplated that a lengthy spell in prison for murder might just be worth it.

The marathon trek with the gear took me twenty sweat stained minutes and by that time the crowd were drifting in. The band was there already. The MC was also their singer, and drums and keyboards made up the trio.

"You're cutting it a bit fine, aren't you?" Snapped the singer, who had been sitting in a chair watching me struggle up and down with my gear. "Give us your dots, (music) you're on in ten minutes."

I hurriedly got changed into my stage gear and waited for my call.

"Well tonight ladies and gentlemen, we have a new face in the club, his name is Brian Flockhart and he does a lot of the songs that I sing, so don't be too hard on him and give him a chance… Brian Flockhart!"

Listening to him singing the warm up numbers with his band, I didn't feel in the slightest worried about my chances with the crowd. He was what you might call, a big-headed bastard, stuck up his own arse. I got through the first spot reasonably well, albeit the organist wasn't exactly playing what was written on the music. This came to a head in the dressing room at the break.

"Your music's all wrong," our impresario said, and producing a pen, he was in the process of scribbling all over my music sheets which I had paid good money to be transposed by a professional.

In no uncertain terms I told him where that pen was going if he so much as touched the sheet music. This left an uneasy atmosphere between myself, the MC and the keyboard player. The one friendly shining light was the drummer, Dave, who was watching this with great delight.

"Those two think they are God's gift around here," he whispered when they stormed out of the room in a temper.

The second half went really well, despite the organist trying deliberately to put me off with some weird backing. After my encore, came the time to thank everyone. (As you do.)

"Ladies and gentlemen," I began, "you've been a wonderful audience (true), I'd like to thank all those involved in running this great club, especially your man on the door who has proved to me that with a very limited intelligence you can be placed in a position of authority."

The audience clapped enthusiastically, which made me realise the irony was not getting through somehow.

"And finally, I'd like to thank the band, on drums we have Dave, come on, give him a big hand!" (More enthusiastic clapping.)

"Thank you, and…. goodnight!" As I left the stage, the stunned look on the MC's and organist's faces was priceless.

Dave came into the dressing room. He had tears streaming down his face.

"That was fucking awesome!" He giggled "I've been waiting for years to see those two wankers get what was coming to them!"

I packed my gear and moaned to Dave about the long haul to the car.

"No, it's dead easy, you just go out the back-stage door, down three steps, and the door in front of you leads out onto the Main Street."

I smiled sweetly and asked where I might

find the doorman. "Who, oh, old Harry, he's long gone home." (Pity.)

This was a pretty dark time for me as a solo artiste. I was in a surreal situation whereas I would be under the glare of the spotlights, performing in front of lots of people who generally enjoyed what I was doing for them, and receiving the applause that it merited, only to dread the journey home to an empty house where I would sit and cry my eyes out, pining for my beloved Tracey.

To anyone who has been in that situation it seemed to me that God was playing funny tricks on us.

On one of these journeys home, it seemed like any other when, while sitting at the traffic lights to turn green, a stunning blonde flung open my passenger door and jumped in. I could see she was in a very agitated state.

"Please help me!" She pleaded. "There's a man following me and I'm scared." Just then the lights changed so I drove off. I calmed her down and asked where I could drop her off.

"If you could let me out a bit farther up the road that would be fine," she said. She asked me where I'd been and I told her I had been gigging in the clubs.

"Oh, that must be great to do that; I suppose you are heading home to the little woman now are you?" She asked.

"No, I live on my own." I replied.

She smiled sweetly. "Perhaps if you have time you would like some company, would you like to come back to my place for a drink so I can thank you for saving me?"

I had been on my own for quite a while since Tracey's death and the offer from this gorgeous girl was too good to turn down. I eagerly accepted.

"Right then," she said in an abrupt business-like manner. "Its fifty quid for a blow job, one hundred quid for full sex, and two hundred for the night!"

I looked at her, stunned. Trust me to pick up a fucking prostitute! I told her in no uncertain terms that I wasn't interested and looked for a place to drop her off. Just ahead was a bus stop with a big queue waiting for the late-night bus.

"Right!" I said, pulling up alongside it. "Out you get!" My fair maiden's mood changed dramatically.

"What are you, some Nancy boy, a fucking queer, can't get it up eh!" She exploded, as I tried to wrestle the car door shut. This caused extreme embarrassment to me and a great deal of amusement to the waiting crowd. I finally managed to slam the door shut and drove off at speed with her still shouting abuse at me. That night in the house I was even lonelier and more dejected than ever.

Tracey's mum had helped me out more than I could have ever imagined after Tracey died. She would look after Becky at the weekends while I carried on singing in the clubs. During the week, Becky stayed with me.

A few years later, once Becky had started primary school, I recall an incident when a small girl was teasing her in the playground at the school. "You've not got a mummy!" She sneered. I was impressed with how Becky handled it. Instead of crying, she just turned around and said, "Yeah, but I've got two beds, two different lots of toys and two TVs! Have you?"

Becky wasn't that much older when her Granny, who had become the mum she never knew, passed away. All this to happen to a girl barely eight years old. Once again, the family stepped in and Brett and Karen took her in as their own and helped me out considerably. It is a fitting testament to their love and affection, to know that Becky has grown into a happy and successful young woman with an managerial position in the licensing trade.

As for myself, I had spent a few years on my own, with a few casual flings here and there. But finally, after all of the darkness, there was a light at the end of tunnel as far as love was concerned. Ironically, it came about as a blind date.

My mate Dave from work had arranged a bowling match so that Becky could meet his daughter who was of a similar age. His wife Debs had also invited her friend, Janet and her little boy Ross to come along as well. Needless to say it was a set up and we quickly fell in love. Sixteen years down the line, we are still together and happy. (Even though my messy habits drive her nuts!)

Bringing up a young child as a single male parent wasn't that easy as any trip we made if she needed the toilet, I would have to ask any random woman at the door to take her in. The age difference didn't help either, with me being over fifty. This was evident many times when I took her out to play on the park at Clitheroe Castle.

I would be sitting on the bench watching her play and without fail, the young mothers there would be watching me with suspicious eyes. In an attempt to show that I was there in all innocence, I would shout, "Here Becky, come to daddy." This was ignored by my daughter every time. (Little sod!)

After at least four attempts to get her to come over to me, I could see the ladies discussing who would fetch the police. (Every time!) When I approached the ladies in question and showed them a photo of myself and my darling daughter, (little sod!) together, their scathing looks turned to little "ooh" and "aah" noises and I was looked at in a new light.

Chapter Twenty-Nine
Back in a band again

I had been performing solo for over three years and I was becoming weary of it all. Although I was doing really well with the crowds and the money was good, I was tired of the treatment that solo acts usually received from the committees. It had got that bad for me, that I bought myself a little mini television to sit and watch in the dressing rooms rather than socialise with anyone running the clubs.

It was about this time that Keith returned from Germany permanently. While we were sitting having a drink one evening, he suggested we might start up a proper band together. This was just the incentive I needed to finish up my solo career and though there would be no real money in it, I jumped at the chance.

We started asking around to recruit members and found a really good guitarist named Steve. My mate Andy worked in the archives in Clitheroe castle and gave us a room to rehearse. (Not many bands can say they rehearsed in a castle!)

As the weeks and rehearsals went by and our list of numbers grew, it was time to find a drummer. It seems strange now, but at the time we had only one guy in mind and it didn't occur to us that he might not be available. As it was, when we approached him, he had just packed up with a band and was free to join and so Dave made up our foursome called "Kickstart."

As a local band in the area, we were definitely a weird mixture. There was Dave on drums. He was from Italian descent and insisted on counting us in in Italian (uno, duo, etc) until we convinced him that English would be better.

Keith, who hailed from Liverpool, myself from Scotland, and Steve, although born and bred in Clitheroe, had spent years travelling the world in the merchant navy.

Our very first gig as Kickstart was at a charity benefit for the Barrow village committee, in aid of funds for the local community. The event was held in a large marquee on a field behind the two pubs. (Memories of that drunken night of the pub crawl came flashing back to me.) As the locals had got to know me for my solo work, they'd asked me if I would do a set during the evening. This was it, our first proper gig and playing to a lot of friends that I had got to know very well since I'd first arrived in Lancashire. All went well and the new band went down a treat.

Later that week, one of the organisers had sent in an article to the local Clitheroe Advertiser newspaper. "Many thanks to Brian Flockhart and the Kickstarts" read the headline. Luckily the rest of the band saw the funny side. I was very happy with how that first gig had gone and was pleased to be part of a group again.

We sounded good and although we wanted to play mainly rock numbers, my old agent gave us gigs in the clubs where sixties and seventies music was very popular.

This was great as far as I was concerned as I no longer had to rely on the dreaded club backing. Steve on the other hand was not very fond of the club scene, and his pet hate was the inevitable bingo which ruled the format for the night.

Nothing riled him more than to be dictated as to when to play or stop, depending on "bingo time." On one occasion we even had the bingo machine bolted to the front and middle of the stage completely in our way.

We had a way of getting some small revenge against those cursed machines. On the older models there was a long clear plastic tube which was the outlet for the balls. They would be sucked up the tube, and at the top was a wire guard which was just wide enough to stop the ball from escaping, and also allowing the bingo caller pick it out. When no one was looking we would bend the guard back and when the machine was started up, the balls would fly up in the air and scatter everywhere.

On every occasion we did this, the caller would try to catch the balls instead of switching off the machine. (Intelligent boy apply within!) Our other trick was to have a spare ball (any number would do) and as the games progressed we would find a committee member and tell him we found this ball in the corner of the dressing room. This would cause a complete uproar as the patrons would demand the games to be played again and the money that had been won, returned. A great amount of time was wasted counting the balls and replaying the games. No one ever suspected us.

After a couple of years doing the club circuit Steve had had enough and decided to call it a day as he never could quite handle the said bingo. We decided to carry on as a trio and although the sound was not as good, we still put in a decent performance.

Some of the venues were more suited to smaller bands and they could be pretty hard work as a few of them had the dreaded sound sensors fitted. These ingenious devices were supposed to make sure the bands volume didn't exceed the desired level, but as they could be set by the clubs, they sometimes beggared belief as to how low they had been set. On one occasion we actually set one off by just walking on to the stage!

Although we had always gone down well with the audiences there is always one or two gigs that don't live up to your expectations. The first I remember was soon after Steve had left. We had been booked to play in Cleater Moor in Cumbria by a different agent. I had played there a few times with the Mimics and had found the audience very hard to please. As Kickstart, we were only going to play music and not have any comedy involved. I thought it would be okay.

Arriving at the front door I was met by the doorman. He was about six foot three, covered in tattoos and wearing bike leathers with chains and studs all over his jacket.

"What music do you play?" He barked. When I told him that it was mainly sixties and seventies pop songs he stared hard at me.

"That's shit! Don't you play any Led Zeppelin, or AC-DC?"

I shook my head.

"Fucking rubbish," he muttered and walked away.

More trouble was to follow when one of the committee asked us why there were only the three of us instead of four. I explained that the agent knew that there was only three of us when he booked us.

"We always have four-piece bands as a rule." He moaned. After all that, the night went surprisingly well and we even played to encores at the end. Thinking nothing more about it, we packed up and headed home.

The next day a very agitated agent called me. "You have to give half the money back!" He pleaded. When I asked why, he said that the club had been on to him, saying that we had been the worst band that had ever played there. I couldn't believe my ears and told him of the two encores that we had, but he was insisting that we pay the club back. This infuriated me. I demanded the telephone number of the club so I could speak directly.

Ten minutes later, I got through to the entertainment's secretary. "What's all this about being rubbish?" I yelled down the phone.

"That's just what you are, Big Harry said so!" He snapped.

"Would that be the prick at the door?" When he confirmed that it was said prick, I asked him if he had noticed the encores that we had been asked for.

"Oh, I wasn't here, I was at a darts match in the next town!"

Shaking my head, I replaced the receiver in its cradle.

Another occasion occurred when the local agent called Pete Barton wanted us for a gig at a Haven holiday camp in Sussex. Pete was handling bands such as The Animals and was highly respected. He also, at times, could bend the truth. (As all agents do!) He wanted us for this gig, but we would be taking the place of another band. (The name escapes me.) We were to say that we were that band, and to make things easier for us, we only had to do about ten numbers. After checking our set-list, he narrowed the ten numbers down, telling us that they would do the business for us. Knowing Pete, he would have got the band we were

Taking the place of, a better gig.

Arriving at the Haven camp, we were overwhelmed by the welcome we received. A gang of guys insisted on lugging all our gear in for us, and the manager was so excited to have us there. (Obviously they hadn't seen the band we were supposed to be!)

"It's going to be a great night!" He chirped. "It's the caravan owners party night, and there will be about six hundred here tonight, all dressed up in their Glam-Rock outfits!"

"Eh?" I said.

"Yes, it's Glam-Rock themed night, that's why we booked you."

Peter, (the swine) had booked the only band who didn't play one glam rock number in their entire set!

I had to come clean with the poor guy and tell him the truth. His face took on a wild, panicked look. "What am I going to do, they will kill me!"

I calmed him down and suggested that he tell the crowd that the band he had booked had broken down somewhere, and at the last minute, he had managed to get a band to step in at short notice. (Us.)

This he announced just before we went on to this dressed-up audience and although there was disappointment in the room, they soon forgot and danced merrily away. There was only one arse-hole, who stood at the side of the stage dressed in a spangly vest, satin trousers, high-boots and a green glitter wig, who kept screaming, "you're shit! You're shit!"

I let him have his rant for a while before I finally snapped back at him.

"You think we are shit? Look at you! You're at least fifty and you're dressed like a tit! Fuck off!". The message got though.

Everyone (except tit!) Enjoyed the night, and a very relieved manager thanked us over and over again, for saving the day.

When we got back to Clitheroe, there was Pete in the pub waiting for us. "You bastard!" I yelled.

"What's wrong?" He said, "I didn't get anybody complaining, so it must have gone down well!" (Sigh, bloody agents.)

After another year or so even we had had enough of the hassle and decided we would just go for the pub scene. This worked out really well as Steve, knowing the bingo was a thing of the past, happily joined forces again. You can never get big headed in this game because sure as hell there will be an instance that will bring you back down to earth.

A classic example happened a few years later, as we by this time had built up a very good reputation around the bars in the area. We were booked into a bar in Blackburn and the host was extremely excited to have us there.

"I've been trying to get you guys here for

ages," he gushed. We put on a show of modesty while basking in his adulation.

"Could I possibly announce you when you start, it would mean soooo much to me! I've been telling everyone about you since we were lucky enough to book you."

We, acting as though we received this treatment wherever we went, graciously agreed. Came the hour, and instruments ready, we called over the host to announce us.

"Ladies and gentlemen, as promised, here they are, please welcome on stage… Jumpstart!"

We all looked at him with puzzled expressions.

"It's Kickstart you prick!" I hissed in his ear.

"Oh yes, sorry about that, Kickstart!" (Sigh.)

The music scene in Clitheroe and the surrounding areas was buzzing at this time. Although Clitheroe was quite a small town, there was plenty of live music in the Kings Arms pub, The Dog, The Commercial, The Craven Heifer, Cross Keys and the Social Club.

Sadly, only the Cross Keys remains, although it's better known these days as Key Street. Two more pubs have taken up the fight to carry on having live music in the town in recent years. There is the Rose and Crown, run by a dynamic landlady called Michelle, and the Buck Inn, run by the equally dynamic Sharon. (God

Bless these two ladies.)

The Kings Arms especially was the pub to play in at the time. They had bands playing on a Friday and a Saturday and the place was always packed. The landlord was a man called Jack and he and his lovely wife had run the pub very successfully for many years. When he retired there was a couple of unsuccessful hosts until Lee and Denise from Bolton took over.

Lee was a giant of a man with a long ponytail. He would sit on his stool behind the bar and converse with the locals, while Denise would make sure all other aspects of the pub ran smoothly. One of her brainwaves still makes me laugh. Kids were allowed in the pub on Sunday afternoons and Denise would offer the kids a prize for the one who collected the most litter from inside and outside the pub. In just ten minutes, the whole place was spotless and all for a packet a crisps!

The only drawback to playing at the Kings Arms was the fact that the stage area for bands was in front of the door to the gents! This meant that poor Keith would be half way through a complicated guitar solo, when he would be shoved to one side by someone wishing to empty his bladder of umpteen pints! Even after a refurb a few years later, which gave alternative access to the toilets that bypassed the stage area, you would still get idiots wading through the gear and Keith, on a direct mission to the urinal, like elephants on their ancestral track to their watering hole.

The Dog Inn on the other hand was laid out much better until some lunatic decided to shift the bands to an adjacent wall to some poor guy's house. This guy was a saint, as every band night he would take all of his ornaments off the shelves to save them from shaking off. He would then put them all back the following morning! The Dog is now a sports bar and the Kings Arms is boarded up, awaiting either new hosts or, what is probably more likely, to be turned into flats.

The good thing nowadays is the smoking ban in the pubs. Before this new law came in, you would come home from a gig and when you woke up in the morning, you would reek of stale cigarette smoke. The worst experience of this was the Golden Cross in Oswaldtwistle. (Gladly no more!) It was a bit of a rough joint and its owners had obviously never heard of extractor fans. Whenever you played, there was a blue haze of tobacco smoke so dense that it was as thick as smog.

As for the Golden Crosses clientele, let's just say that they were sadly lacking in social skills. On one occasion, just as we were setting up, I was approached by a drunken, wild-eyed madman.

"Oasis! I want you to play Oasis!" He screamed, spraying me with spittle, his face just inches away from mine. When I informed him that we didn't play any Oasis numbers, he was not in the least impressed. "Well then you are fucking shit! You hear me? Shit!"

As soon as we began playing our first set, he sprang up from his seat and stood in front of me yelling obscenities. Eventually, the bar staff had him removed. As he was being man-handled out of the door, we broke into a Rolling Stones number.

That's it!" He bellowed. "That's Oasis!" (My defence rests.)

On the whole though we didn't meet up with too many hitches. As we moved into the early millennium we wanted to try a new venue outlet and my brother Tom came up with the idea of bringing the band up to my native neck of the woods for a gig.

Now, knowing my dear brother, you could guarantee there would be some catch or other about it. He booked us in to the "Faside Inn" which was in a mining village called Wallyford. (Not quite Wembley Stadium.)

The "Faside," if you'll forgive me for saying, was not quite the most select watering hole you might find when I lived in those parts, but brother Tom assured me that it had been revamped and was okay. On his word we took the booking and to cover the expenses I managed to get a further booking for the following night in Edinburgh.

Brother had booked a caravan for the rest of the band and wives and my mate Andy was staying with me at my dad's house. I hired a cheap van, so everything was set for our Scottish adventure.

As we drove through Wallyford my heart sank as I looked across the road to the site of the "Faside." Nothing had changed apart from the sign had disappeared from the front and the paintwork had gotten even shoddier!

"Look at that shithole!" Steve chortled, "You wouldn't catch me dead in that place!"

My face must have said it all as he turned to me in disbelief.

"You are fucking kidding me!" He yelled. I muttered something about it being really nice inside and not to judge a book by its cover. The rest of the band thought it was hilarious. (But not the wives.)

The caravan was a little better, but we really should have booked two as it was pretty cramped for six people. The positive side was that Tom had done the business and sold out the gig.

After getting the ladies settled in the caravan we went back to set up the gear. Inside, the pub was about the same as I had remembered it. Well-worn carpets and smoke-stained wallpaper. There were even the same people, be it a little older, sitting in the same seats at the bar.

Steve was definitely not impressed even when we went into the function room which was a lot better. (No carpets to wear down and a lick of paint applied in the last five years.)

After we had set up and I had run out of apologies, we returned to our digs with a sense of foreboding. This wasn't eased when Andy and I got a taxi to the gig.

"Where you going pal?" Our driver asked.

"Faside Inn please," I answered.

"The Faside! Are you sure about that?!" He persisted. "Rather you than me mate, good luck!"

Andy and I looked at each other like condemned men.

It turned out to be a cracking night as all of the audience were old friends and people who remembered me from my cabaret days. As people will tell you, if a Scottish audience like you, you will know about it. I spent a pleasant hour or so after the gig catching up with those old friends and even Steve grudgingly admitted that he had had a good time.

The following evening, we set off for the B.M.C. club for our second gig in high spirits, ready to rock their socks off. The first thing that put us off was the climb with the gear up to the main function room.

Once set up we were told that this was to be an "experimental" try out as they had only used traditional bands up to that point. (Waltzes, quickstep, etc.)

The only trouble with that was that the committee hadn't bothered to inform the audience about the change. As they trooped in you could see the look of concern on their faces as they observed the large amount of amplifiers and guitars spread over the stage. No sooner had we launched into our first number, when they began to trickle out of the hall with disapproving looks cast in our direction.

As the night progressed the trickle became a flood and before too long there was only one table remaining, with four very angry persons sitting at it. You just knew, that rather than join the rest of the crowd downstairs in the lounge (which was packed to capacity by this time!) they were going to sit it out to the bitter end and give us as much grief as possible.

Their spokesman came over and demanded we play a waltz. "You're shite!" He barked when we said we didn't do waltzes.

"Well, how about a highland Scotteesh?" He continued. (Excuse the spelling for anybody who knows what the hell it was!) Having got another negative reply he stormed off back to his table, telling the other three what a pile of dung we were. Ten minutes later he was back.

"Do ye no do any Jennifer Rush?" He pleaded. Even when I tried to explain in layman terms that we were an all-male band and that

Jennifer was a female, which would make it pretty impossible to sing her songs unless one of us had his balls cut off, this did nothing to appease him and he stormed off once more back to his friends.

At the break I made a bee line to his table in a pretty foul mood.

"Can I ask you how old you are?" I enquired.

"I'm forty-five, why?" He answered.

"Forty-five going on ninety if you ask me!" I hissed. Even that couldn't shift the dreaded foursome and they sat there enjoying our embarrassment as the night seemed to last forever. About an hour before the end we decided we had had enough and sarcastically thanked the audience and bade them goodnight.

We hadn't even taken the guitars from around our necks when a group of committee men surrounded us by the stage.

"What's going on here?" One of them demanded.

"Look, it's plain to see that your little experiment hasn't worked, so, I think in the circumstances we should wrap it up and call it a day." I said.

"Oh no laddie, you are booked for another hour yet and another hour you will play!" He snorted. Realising that to argue would be futile, we strapped our instruments on again and carried on playing to our hostile foursome.

With the gear in the van and our fee grudgingly handed over by a frosty man in charge of the club's finance, we set off back to the caravan park to drink and wind down from the experience. (It was going to take a lot of drink!)

The others had gone on ahead to buy takeaways which left Keith, big Andy and myself in the van. We were just beginning to see the funny side of the experience when the van ground to a halt. After unsuccessfully trying the starter a few times, we sat and thought out our next course of action.

"Try it again," said Keith after a few minutes. Surprisingly, the engine roared into life. On we travelled once more. Exactly one mile later the damn thing spluttered to a halt once again. We sat and waited for a few minutes again, and once again the engine burst into life.

This carried on for the whole journey which should have taken half an hour but ended up taking over three and a half. The final stop was only thirty yards from the camp site, and as the road was right beside the sea you could hear the waves gently breaking over the rocks.

I commented on this to Keith who gave me such a murderous look that I decided not to pursue the topic any further. After a meal of cold pizza and chips, and being asked what took us so long, big A and I made our retreat and headed home.

The next morning we managed to get a breakdown mechanic to fix the problem.

"This is a hired van then is it?" He asked. When I nodded he shook his head.

"It's a fucking death trap if you ask me, shouldn't be on the road!"

I decided to keep that information from the rest of them (especially Keith) and we set off home to Lancashire.

Chapter Thirty
Parting of the ways

In our tenth year together as a band, our drummer Dave gave us the bad news that he was going to emigrate to Australia. This hit the rest of us hard as we were not only in a band together but were firm and close friends as well. (Not too often found in bands as a rule.)

Even as he made final preparations for his leaving I still clung on to the vain hope that he would change his mind and stay. Sadly, it was not to be and we got together for the last time to see him on his journey to his new life.

We were not out of gigging for long as Alan, my mate from Scotland, stepped in to help us out. We knew that this could only be a temporary situation as it cost him more to travel down than what we could pay him! (I think he did it out of love.)

The situation was soon resolved, as Tony, a local lad, stepped in to take over. Things settled down and we went on as before, playing around the area and doing mainly the pub circuit.

About a year or so after Tony joined we were invited to do an open air concert for charity in the grounds of Clitheroe castle. This was so successful that it was staged again the following year. Whereas, on the previous year it had run smoothly, the second time was not the case.

As is always the case in recent years, there appears the dreaded "health and safety" lesser spotted Neanderthal. This particular specimen was a prince among their princes. With only five hours before the start of the concert he had decided that the extension to the stage was not sturdy enough and would need to be reinforced. (Having had at least two months previously to plan this.)

This delayed our sound check to the point that left us five minutes to test it out. Tony and I had been asked to get there early and had waited almost the entire five hours and had only less than half an hour to get home and change without any time for a meal.

On my return there were fire exit signs attached to the front of the stage pointing the way to a narrow exit path on the right-hand side. Considering that the venue was an open-air, concrete amphitheatre with no combustibles, I thought it the most stupidest of ideas, as almost two thousand people would be there, and if by any chance there was a fire and by any chance they were daft enough to follow the exit signs, they would all be crushed to death in the ensuing stampede. This as you can imagine, did not enamour me to the man, but worse was yet to follow.

We had just finished our spot to a rapturous applause and had stripped our gear off the stage before the last band was setting up, thinking we could make a quick getaway to the pub. With my car loaded I went to find the sound engineer to move his van to let me out.

After waiting for ten minutes for him to arrive I went back to see what the problem was.

"I'm not allowed to move it," he said.

"Why?" I asked.

"That guy over there says it could be dangerous with all these people around," he answered.

There he was, looking very important in his high visibility vest. I approached him in a seething mood.

"Look, I've got over two thousand pounds worth of equipment in the back of my car, which is an estate with side windows for all the world to see what's inside and two thousand people in the park, with a probable two percent who would quite easily nick what they could, so I need to get it home."

"You're not moving that car, there's too many people around," the jobs-worth replied stubbornly.

"They are all watching the concert you prick!" I exploded. We argued for a few minutes but it was a futile task as he was adamant that nothing was moving while the concert was on.

Giving up in exasperation I went home for some food. I returned just as the concert was ending to see this prize idiot backing a car down the lane with throngs of people heading home in its way. He looked quite startled as I approached him. (To be fair, I did look as though I was going to kill him.)

"Making sure everything is safe, are we?!" I exploded, and without waiting for his lame excuse I jumped in my car and followed the car he was ushering down the lane. If ever a man was in the wrong job, he would have been given first prize.

Shortly after this, Alan came up with the suggestion that we should play at the Edinburgh Festival. Keith, Steve, and myself were really keen to do it, but it meant that Tony would miss out as it was Alan's idea. Tony told us that he was okay about it, although I think he would have loved to have played there.

For those who don't know about it, the Edinburgh Festival is known throughout the world for its "fringe" entertainment which lasts the whole of August. Many "stars" past and present have been discovered whilst performing there, so I thought, why not us. Stranger things have happened at sea as they say.

Alan managed to get us booked into a venue called "Whistle Binkies" (strange name but true.) This club put on four bands per night, seven nights a week, all year long and was one of the top spots in Edinburgh just situated off the Royal Mile.

On the night of the gig and wearing my new t-shirt with the logo, "karaoke, Japan's revenge for Hiroshima!" emblazoned on the front, we took to the stage.

Now, as I said, the festival was known worldwide and people from all over said world would descend upon Edinburgh in their thousands, it probably was an oversight on my part that there may be a few of these people from Japan.

What I didn't expect was the first three rows in the packed club were all Japanese! As the gig wore on, I was conscious of the attention that was being paid to me by them. At the end of the gig I was surrounded by some of them, all jabbering away at me in a very excited state.

As I tried to calm the situation by apologising profusely, one of the ringleaders grabbed my arm.

"Where we can buy your t-shirt?" he asked!

We returned the following year and had a similar success to the previous one, but we could see that Steve was tiring of the gigging and his heart was not in it any more. It was only a matter of time before he announced that he was giving the band up. I think he missed playing with Dave and the closeness that the band had had, so, after sixteen years together, he called it a day.

Surprisingly, even in a small town like Clitheroe, there were an abundance of musicians, and Steve's place was filled by Jim who was a very competent player.

And so, the band carried on with the two "new" members for a couple of years more. It was obvious that Jim and Tony had other musical interests such as jazz and blues and even when we returned to Edinburgh for our third time at the "fringe" with Jim, it didn't seem to impress him as much as I thought it would.

The telltale signs became more obvious as they branched out to play with other outfits while still with our band and once again there came a parting of the ways and Keith and I were left to try and carry on.

As in many times before, just when I thought my "career" as a player was coming to an end, fate stepped in. I was in the garage owned by my long-suffering partner Janet's brother, Andrew. (Janet, who has put up with me for over sixteen years!) and bemoaning the fact that we were once again on the lookout for new members, when he disappeared and returned with his phone.

"Here, speak to this guy, his name is Chris," he said. Apparently, Andrew had known Chris for a long time and knew he played guitar with a number of well-known bands in the area. He had only spoken to him recently because he had crashed his Land rover and it was in for a major repair!

"I don't think I'd be any good for you," Chris said. "I'm nearly seventy-years old!"

"I wouldn't worry about that," I said. "I

am nearly seventy-one!"

A meeting was arranged at his house with Keith and myself and our guitars, to see how it went. It couldn't have gone better and the icing on the cake came in the form of Dec, a top-class drummer who we had known for many years, (and tried to get him to join once or twice,) had worked with Chris and agreed to join as well.

So, there we were, back on the road again, as the old song says. It has to be said that the present line up of the band is as good as we have had for a while (no disrespect to Tony, or Jim) and we have continued for two years.

Unfortunately, the gigs are becoming harder to get as pubs and clubs are closing down at an alarming rate, and the new tack seems to be to have an "open night" where musicians get up on stage for a few numbers for a free beer or two.

Although you have to see the venue's point of view, it still saddens me that there are so many great talents out there who will never get the chance to get any further.

As the number of gigs and venues slowly diminished, I found myself with extra time on my hands. It was my friend Peter Wareing who got me back into doing extras TV work again. He was with an agency in Manchester called Industry Castings, and when I mentioned that I had done some work previously, he suggested that I take it up again.

It appeared that you didn't have to have an Equity card anymore. (This was good news to me, as if I had to pay my back dues, it would have run into thousands!) I was a bit nervous at the interview, but the main woman Lois put me at ease.

"Just what we are looking for!" She said, "turn around so we can take a photo of the back of your head!"

I know I'm no oil-painting, but surely I'm not that bad-looking. The rear of my head having passed muster, I was signed up on the spot. A few weeks later, I was given my first job. It was in a drama called "The 'A' Word" with Christopher Eccleston. The scene was in a doctor's surgery waiting room and I was cast as a patient waiting for treatment. The director approached me, "Brian, I want you to pretend to cough, but not to make a sound."

I assured him that I could do a wonderful cough that might get me an Oscar, but he insisted I stay mute. A few weeks later when it was shown on the telly, there I was, coughing as though I was on sixty fags a day. I found out later that if I coughed for real they would have had to pay extra for a speaking part!

It was a few months later before my next job. Lois phoned me to tell me that Peter Kay had picked me for Car Share, one of the most popular programmes on TV at the time. I had to get there at short notice for six-thirty in the evening. There were only four extras on the set and as we were getting to know one another, Peter arrived and asked if we had been fed.

The other extras lived in the Manchester area and had already eaten something. But I piped up and said I was starving.

"Follow me, our kid!" He said, and took me outside to the mobile canteen in the yard.

"Yes Mr Kay?" Said the caterer.

"Fill that plate lad!" Said Peter and walked away with a generous portion. When I stood by the counter the caterer's attitude changed completely.

"What do you want?" He snapped.

"I'll have the same as my mate, Peter, if you don't mind." I replied.

We were filming in a junk-yard, in a bus-stop (don't ask me why, it was the co-star Sian's dreamscape.) Peter did everything, behind the camera, setting up shots, sound etc. When the plastic at the back of the bus shelter reflected into the camera, he was up there helping the crew to rip it off.

Sian and Peter were best mates from a long way back and it showed with the banter between them. "Sian," Peter said, "try to look attractive, you know, beautiful."

"You first, you fat bastard!" She replied.

After the first take, Peter shouted out that it was great. I had visions of heading home early. This idea was dashed as one of the engineers said, "You're working with Peter Kay, he's a perfectionist, you've no chance of going home early!"

True to his word, and endless takes later, Peter was finally satisfied that we looked miserable enough to call it a wrap, and in the early hours of the morning I set off for home.

Shortly after Megan from the agency called me for a stint on Coronation Street. This brought great excitement to Janet's mum Sheila, who was an avid fan. On the day of the shoot, I had only a quick walk on part, and was told to "walk with purpose." The whole thing took two seconds. I had told her what the producer had said to me, and when it was aired she commented on how I had walked really purposely well!

A shoot with Sean Bean in a detective serial called Broken was next. It was filmed in a pub in a rough district of Liverpool as we sat in the bar next to the lounge where it was being shot, I noticed two small holes in the glass window where I was sitting. "Bit of a turf war going on here," said one of the locals. "Decided to put the frighteners up us by firing a couple of shots through that window," he continued. Just then my pal Peter arrived and I very generously insisted that he had my seat!

Since then I have had jobs on Emmerdale, Victoria, the film Peterloo, Bancroft, City and The City, Coldfeet, where I was asked to grow a week's worth of stubble as I was playing a homeless man. (Typecast!) On the shoot I was filmed walking out the door with my back to the camera. (Ah that rear of my head photo came in handy!)

My most recent extra work was on Peaky Blinders where I spent almost three days in a fight scene. This got quite dangerous as some of the cast were taking it very seriously and had a few bruises to prove it. (Me included.) Contrary to belief, there is never much money in it as it is taken up with agency fees and expenses, but I still find it fun on the whole and I always get to meet some great characters and I am always standing by the phone waiting for the next extras job to come in.

As I have looked back over the last fifty-five years in this book, I feel blessed that I was able to perform and play through so many changes in the musical decades. A major regret is missing out on my two sons Paul and Bryan growing up while I worked away from home but at least we still have a special bond and they still love their old dad. (Especially around Christmas!) Paul is quite content with his life in Musselburgh and Bryan has a very successful band in Edinburgh. (A chip of the old block maybe?)

Do I regret not quite making it to the big time? (Of course I do!!!) But then again, I'm still playing.

In closing, I'd like to apologise to the people who I have not included in my story, and to some whom I have changed the names (to protect the guilty!) and a big thank you to Janet (the long suffering one) for suggesting I write this book after listening to my many tales (over and over again!)

Who knows, maybe next year, I'll be famous.

THE END

Printed in Great Britain
by Amazon